W9-AQE-658

Ask Peter Kreeft

Peter Kreeft

Ask Peter Kreeft

The 100 Most Interesting Questions He's Ever Been Asked

SOPHIA INSTITUTE PRESS
Manchester, New Hampshire

Copyright © 2019 by Peter Kreeft

Printed in the United States of America. All rights reserved.

Cover design by Perceptions Design Studio.

On the cover: vintage microphone (280987793)
© Oleg Krugliak / Shutterstock.

Unless otherwise noted, Scripture quotations are taken from the Revised Standard Version of the Bible: Catholic Edition, copyright © 1965, 1966 the Division of Christian Education of the National Council of the Churches of Christ in the United States of America. Used by permission. All rights reserved.

No part of this book may be reproduced, stored in a retrieval system, or transmitted in any form, or by any means, electronic, mechanical, photocopying, or otherwise, without the prior written permission of the publisher, except by a reviewer, who may quote brief passages in a review.

Sophia Institute Press
Box 5284, Manchester, NH 03108
1-800-888-9344

www.SophiaInstitute.com

Sophia Institute Press® is a registered trademark of Sophia Institute.

Library of Congress Cataloging-in-Publication Data
Names: Kreeft, Peter, author.
Title: Ask Peter Kreeft : the 100 most interesting questions he's ever been aked / Peter Kreeft.
Description: Manchester : Sophia Institute Press, 2019. | Summary: "Answers to a hundred questions—on philosophy, religion, morality, culture, and other topics—that people have asked author Peter Kreeft"—Provided by publisher.
Identifiers: LCCN 2019025006 | ISBN 9781622828609 (paperback)
Subjects: LCSH: Theology—Miscellanea. | Catholic Church—Doctrines—Miscellanea. | Philosophy—Miscellanea
Classification: LCC BR118 .K695 2019 | DDC 230—dc23
LC record available at https://lccn.loc.gov/2019025006

First printing

Contents

Introduction xiii

Philosophy

What is philosophy good for? What can I do with it? 3

Who are your favorite philosophers? 7

Why are so many philosophers weird? 9

Who was the first Christian philosopher? 11

Where do your thoughts come from? 13

Can you tell us a piece of wisdom from your father? 21

Which do you think is more dangerous: optimism
or pessimism? Naivete or cynicism and suspicion? 23

You've been criticized as "simplistic."
How do you respond to that? 25

Can you give us some really simple,
practical, advice? 29

God

Why do you have to bring God into everything? 33

What is your favorite proof for the existence of God? 35

Does God have a sense of humor? 39

Prayer and Meditation

What is your favorite method of prayer? 45

Do you recommend meditation exercises? 47

What methods do you recommend for prayer and
meditation? 49

How do you meditate? 51

What about us busy people who don't
have time for meditation? 55

Religion

What do you think is the origin of religion? 61

Why are there more women than men in church? 65

Why are there more old people than young people in
church? 67

What can we do for the cause of reunion
of all the churches? 69

I think Muslims are our number-one enemies.
What do you think? 71

Are we losing our religious freedom? 75

Catholicism

Why are you a Catholic? 79

What Mass do you go to?. 83

You say that God is all good, all wise, and all powerful.
Does that mean that this must be really "the best of all
possible worlds"? 85

If you were pope, what is the first thing you would do? . . . 89

If you were a priest and your parish was dying,
what would you do about it? 91

Why is the Eucharist central? 93

What's the reason for all the fuss you Catholics
make about Mary? 97

How can Protestants and Catholics understand
one another better when we think of Mary?. 103

Why does the Church resist women's ordination? 105

Marriage and Sexuality

What is marriage and why is it so great? 109

Why not trial marriages—living together? 111

Why does the Catholic Church forbid divorce? 113

Why won't the Church allow divorced and remarried
Catholics to receive the Eucharist? 115

How can I tell if I love someone? 121

We're both sexually addicted and sexually confused.
What is sex?. 123

Why is the Catholic Church obsessed with sex?. 125

What's the essence of the Theology of the Body? 129

Why are children important?. 131

Why is the Catholic Church the only church
that forbids birth control? 133

What's the difference between NFP and contraception? . 135

What's wrong with masturbation?. 137

Why do people want to change their gender? 139

Spiritual Life

How can we have joy when our lives are full of misery?. . 143

Isn't the answer just to "let go"? 145

Why do many people today say they are "spiritual"
but not "religious"?. 147

Sin and Evil

Do you believe in Original Sin? 153

What is your solution to the problem of evil? 155

Are there some problems that are impossible to solve? . . 157

What is "the unforgivable sin"? 161

Morality

What *is* right and wrong?. 165

What do we do about imperfections? 167

Do you think Dostoyevsky was right when he said,
"If God does not exist, everything is permissible"?. 169

Does God care more about truth or goodness?. 173

How can we be both just and merciful? 175

How should I vote?. 177

The Supernatural

Why don't we hear anything about angels anymore? . . . 181

What difference do angels make? 185

Have you ever seen an angel? 187

Have you ever seen a ghost? 189

Can a cat be possessed by a demon? 191

Have you ever seen a miracle? 193

Heaven

What will Heaven be like?. 197

What do you think you will do in Heaven? 199

How many people do you think will be in Heaven?. . . . 201

What language will we speak in Heaven? 203

I'm not sure I want to go to Heaven 205

Why don't Catholics believe in reincarnation? 207

Science

Is there a multiverse? 213

Why is there a war between science and religion? 215

Books and Music

What do you love most about the Bible? 221

If you could take only ten books with you to a desert
island for the rest of your life, what would they be? 223

Can fiction be true or false? 227

You've written more than eighty books.
Which of them is your favorite? 229

Tell us one practical thing you've learned
from Chesterton. 231

What are your favorite movies? 233

What do you think about Christian rock? 237

Culture

Why are you countercultural? 241

#79 Which technological invention do you think
is the most dangerous? 243

Are you an optimist or a pessimist about our culture? . . . 245

Can you say something good about
our modern American culture?. 247

What's the most important thing we can do
for our culture? 249

Aren't we too fussy about manners? 251

Why don't people have deep friendships anymore? 253

Don't you think the whole problem is very simple?
We're materialists. 255

What's your favorite joke? 257

Surfing

Do you still surf? 271

What's the big deal about surfing? 273

You're not a surfer; you use a boogie board, a sponge. . . . 275

Miscellany

What is the secret of your success as a writer? 279

In light of your last answer,
don't you believe in autonomy? 285

Does that mean we are dependent? 287

Is BC still Catholic? 289

Would you recommend that I send my kid to BC?. 291

So, is BC Catholic, or is it Jesuit? 293

What is the best college for philosophy? 297

How can we appreciate everything's preciousness? 299

How important are pets? 301

What's the hardest question you were ever asked? 303

About the Author 305

Introduction

"Ask Peter Kreeft"? What a ridiculous title! Who is he, anyway, the Answer Man? Even God refused to be the Answer Man to Job: His "answer" was only more questions.

I didn't choose that arrogant-sounding title; the publisher did. So blame the publisher.

But Sophia Institute Press is a great publisher because they are devoted to Sophia, which means "wisdom." The ancient Greek Sophists claimed to have wisdom; Socrates claimed only to be in love with it, so he called himself not a sophist but a philo-sophist, or philosopher, literally, a lover of wisdom.

I say four cheers for Socrates!

Hardly ever have I heard a lecture (i.e., a monolog) that did not bore me. Hardly ever have I heard a Q & A (i.e., a dialog) that did. That is why Plato, the first and greatest writer of philosophy, wrote in dialogs. No one ever wrote philosophy better than Plato. Wouldn't you think that after 2,400 years, philosophers would learn at least to try to imitate him?

Christians claim to know the ultimate reason for the superiority of dialog over monolog: it is because dialog is one step closer to trialog, which is the nature of ultimate reality, i.e., the Trinity. Monolog is boring. That's why God must be more than one lonely, egotistic, boring divine Person. My favorite argument for the central and most distinctive tenet of Christianity, that Jesus is God in the flesh, is this: Jesus was the only person in history who never bored anyone who met Him. I think that is an even more impressive sign of His divinity than His miracles are.

I give a lot of lectures around the country, in universities and churches, usually to very engaged, thoughtful, curious audiences; and I always make as much time as possible for Q & A afterward.

Here are some of the most interesting questions I have been asked, and my answers. They are essentially the questions I got and the answers I gave in real Q & A sessions, though some of the answers are longer and more leisurely. Speaking is always more time conscious and "under the gun" than writing is. Sometimes I expanded my answers a lot, sometimes a little, sometimes not at all.

They are a mixed bag, as real questions from real people always are. All of them except one or two were asked in Q & A, but not usually word for word: I condensed most of the questions and expanded some of my answers. Some are profound, some silly; some tragic, some funny; some easy, some hard; some simple, some complex.

Enough. The best introductions are the shortest. (My favorite was "Heeeere's Johnny!")

Philosophy

You teach philosophy. Why? What is philosophy good for? What can I do with it?

Nothing. But it can do something with you.

It's like truth, goodness, and beauty that way, and also love, joy, and peace, and also faith, hope, and charity. It's not like money, power, business, consulting, leadership, management, medicine, math, or technology, all of which are practical means to some further end. "Philosophy" means "the love of wisdom," and the love of wisdom implies the wisdom of love, and love and wisdom are both ends, not just means. They are worth doing and having for their own sakes.

What can philosophy do with you? It can open you up, like a coconut, like an egg. You are designed to hatch, to open up. If you don't, you get rotten. Philosophy, like your five bodily senses, leads you out of the dark little prison of yourself into a larger world. It can get you out of Plato's cave, where all you see are shadows.

It can give you the second greatest thing in the world, which is the thirst for the greatest thing in the world. That greatest thing has many names and many attributes. Wisdom and love are two of them.

Really, all those things—wisdom, love, truth, goodness, beauty—are attributes of God. So true philosophy is really the search for God, even if the philosopher doesn't know that and doesn't use that name—in fact, even if the philosopher is an atheist. God is usually present anonymously. He is humble, unlike us.

Augustine implies this divine anonymity when he says, in his *Confessions*, that his conversion began long before he became a Christian, when he became a philosopher by reading Cicero's great exhortation to philosophy, the *Hortensius* (a book that has been lost to history), because he fell in love with eternal wisdom, long before he knew the true God personally and religiously, long before he knew that the thing he loved—wisdom—was to be found in its fullness only in God.

Philosophy will give you the search, the questions. It might even give you some answers, but it will always give you great questions. It will make you a little Socrates, and Socrates can help you to move to the next step, which is to become a little Christ. Philosophy will change you from a pig satisfied to Socrates dissatisfied. And then Socrates can help you begin the journey from Socrates dissatisfied toward Socrates satisfied as Augustine's restless heart and mind were eventually satisfied.

Even if philosophy makes you only dissatisfied and unhappy, it's good. Being unhappy with Brave New World, with Plato's cave, with your pigsty and mud pies—that's progress. In fact, it is necessary. William Barrett, in *Irrational Man*, defends studying Jean-Paul Sartre, probably the most famous nihilist and pessimist in the history of philosophy, this way: "It is better to confront our own existence in despair than never to confront it at all." Despair can be a powerful moment on the road to hope.

Thoreau said: "The mass of men lead lives of quiet desperation." T. S. Eliot called us "hollow men" and said that we "measure out our lives with coffee spoons." There is an alternative: good philosophy, especially classic philosophy. (But not most current academic, scholarly philosophy. Sampling both will show you the difference.)

That's half the answer: the greatness of philosophy, something to be proud of. Here is the other half of the answer, and it's just as important as the first half: that philosophy is something to be humble about; that Socrates was right when he said that the only wisdom is to know you have no wisdom; that there are only two kinds of people: fools, who think they are wise, and the wise, who know they are fools. If Socrates is right, most philosophers are not as wise as farmers and ditch diggers. In fact, philosophers are often nuts. Descartes says, "There is no idea so absurd that it has not been taught by some philosopher." We say in academia about a really ridiculous idea: "That idea could be believed only by a philosopher." Either half of my answer without the other is equally wrong.

I once had a very bright and very sincere student who took a lot of my courses and got straight As in all of them. But I thought he was too serious and lacked a sense of humor. One day, he came to my office in great distress. He said, "I love philosophy. I want to be a philosopher just like you. I've taken all the philosophy courses I can. But I've hit a wall, a crisis, and I don't know who to turn to except you. My crisis is this: philosophy has taught me to question everything, and so now I'm questioning philosophy. Why should I dedicate my whole life to philosophy? What good is it? Tell me. I come to you because you've dedicated your whole life to philosophy, so you must have had a good reason for it. I need to know. Tell me what philosophy means to you. Please!"

He was so troubled and so serious that I thought he needed something more than a straight, serious answer. So I said to him: "Smith (his name was Smith—a very unusual first name), I think

I can answer your question. I have indeed taught philosophy full-time all of my adult life. Do you see all these books? [I had just moved into a newer, larger office, and had four very large bookcases crammed with my books.] The complete works of Plato, Aristotle, Augustine, Boethius, Anselm, Aquinas, Machiavelli, Descartes, Pascal, Bacon, Spinoza, Leibniz, Locke, Berkeley, Hume, Kant, Hegel, Marx, Kierkegaard, Nietzsche, Newman, James, Dewey, Wittgenstein, Russell, Husserl, Heidegger, Sartre, Chesterton, Lewis, Tolkien, Dostoyevsky—I have read all of these books, and I think I can now answer your question."

He was surprised and pleased at my assertion of authority, which I never tra. It was just what he wanted. But it wasn't what he needed. It was a setup.

"I will now tell you what the value of all this philosophy is, Smith. It's nonsense, Smith, it's 99 percent nonsense."

"But ... but if you believe that, how do you go on living? I thought ... I thought the meaning of life was philosophy."

"I have found the real meaning of life, Smith."

"What is it? Tell me!"

"I will do better than that. I will show you." It was summer, and I was going surfing that afternoon, so under my desk I had a bright yellow boogie board. I bought it out, put it on my desk, and said, "There is the meaning of life, Smith. Surfing. The meaning of life is surfing."

It was a risk. He could have slammed the door in righteous anger. Instead, he broke out laughing and went on laughing for a full minute—the first time I had ever heard the wisdom of laughter from his lips.

Someone once asked me whether I thought Heaven was serious or funny. My answer was: That's a very funny question.

Who are your favorite philosophers?

I'll give you three in each historical period, ancient, medieval, and modern: Socrates, Plato, Aristotle; Augustine, Anselm, Aquinas; Pascal, Kierkegaard, and Chesterton. To find out why, read my history of philosophy, *Socrates' Children: The 100 Greatest Philosophers*.

The last three choices are surprising. Do you really think they're the three most important modern philosophers? What about Descartes and Hume and Kant?

You asked me for my personal favorites. Descartes, Hume, and Kant are probably the three most important modern philosophers, and three of the most brilliant. But they're all wrong. Descartes underestimated the body and the senses; Hume underestimated the mind and reason; and Kant put them together backward.

No atheists in your list?

If I were an atheist, I'd rank Lucretius, Nietzsche, and Sartre as the greatest philosophers, the most consistent atheists. Lucretius is a consistent materialist, Sartre a consistent rationalist, and Nietzsche a consistent inconsistentist, or irrationalist. Even if you deeply disagree with them, they are brilliant, and they are fully what they are—as I think an honest atheist would say of my theist picks too.

What do you get out of atheists?

I look at my three atheists as three works of art: you can understand them and admire them even though you don't buy them. And they're three of the best writers among philosophers. Most philosophers are not great writers. All nine of my favorites are.

And, of course, because we are not God, we appreciate things best by contrast: pleasure by pain, life by death, good by evil. I never appreciated my father as much as I did when he died. The same is true of God. To see what difference God makes, read Nietzsche on the death of God. I appreciate theists best by reading atheists. I am grateful to them. I hope they feel the same about me.

Why are so many philosophers weird?

My answer is simple: About 90 percent of all people who have ever lived have had children. About 10 percent of famous philosophers have.

Children are our most effective educators. They keep us sane. They do this by almost driving us insane. If you don't have somebody whom you love so much that he almost drives you insane, it's very hard to be sane.

Children are the answer to the agonized, lonely cry of the sixties hippie, expressed in the popular song line "I need somebody to love."

That's not what the song meant? Oh, sorry. I thought a song was supposed to mean what it said. If it did, then I guess I'm losing my hearing. I thought you said, "I need somebody to love." You really said, "I want somebody to lust."

But lust and love are almost the same thing, aren't they?

Oh sure. Just as selfishness and unselfishness are almost the same thing. Like slavery and freedom, or war and peace.

The world's most effective teachers of morality are having children. Nothing makes your love more unselfish and wholehearted more quickly or more radically than having kids.

Kids teach you just by existing. They demand your time, your love, your advice, your rules, your attention, your money, your mind, and your body. They need you.

The essence — the most rudimentary and universal essence — of all morality is love, charity, altruism, unselfishness, willing the good of others, acting for the good of others. Nobody can ever be a closer "other" for you than each of your kids. Even your spouse is more independent of you than your kids are. Parents are millions of miles ahead of nonparents in learning this morality.

Whenever there is a public vote for any issue that has a moral component, the clearest, most predictable difference is not between Republicans and Democrats, or between conservatives and liberals, or between rich and poor. It's between those who have kids and those who don't.

Parenting also makes the biggest difference in religion. Kids leave religion; parents return. Over half of all Roman Catholics in America today leave the Church before they get married and have kids.

The most common reason for returning is for the kids. Like parachute jumpers, soldiers in foxholes, and big wave surfers, parents know they need God. And for similar reasons.

Who was the first Christian philosopher?

Christ. He loved His Father and what His Father is, and one of the things His Father is, is wisdom, and philosophy is the love of wisdom; therefore, Christ loved wisdom and therefore was a philosopher.

Christ didn't love wisdom because He lacked it but because He had it. You don't love your spouse only when you are courting, but also when you are married. You don't love health only when you are sick but also when you are well. You don't love the sun only on cloudy days.

The first and greatest merely human Christian philosopher was Mary. Her fiat to God contains all of human wisdom in one word.

The first great male Christian philosopher was St. John the Evangelist. Read his Gospel (especially its first chapter) to see his profound and inexhaustible wisdom.

The first labeled, public, career Christian philosopher was St. Justin Martyr, the patron saint of philosophers. Read about his conversion in his two apologies and his *Dialog with Trypho*.

The first and in many ways greatest Christian philosopher was St. Augustine. No one outside of the New Testament influenced the Christian mind more than he.

Ask Peter Kreeft

The most brilliant Christian philosopher who ever lived, and my candidate for simply the most brilliant philosopher who ever lived, is St. Thomas Aquinas. The Church has always put him first for good reasons.

Where do your thoughts come from?

From the same place yours do. We're both human, I think.

But that raises the real question: Where do yours come from? In other words, I will interpret your question universally rather than individually and personally, because I hope you are curious about yourself, not about me. After all, you're not going to have to live with me after this talk is over, but you are going to have to live with yourself for the rest of your life — and that means forever, if 90 percent of all human beings who have ever lived are right and death does not do to your essential self what it does to your body.

OK, let's think seriously and philosophically about that question: Where do thoughts come from?

That's a great question, and one that we probably never asked.

They must come from somewhere. Because they come, they happen, they begin, and nothing just happens without a cause, whether it's an event in the history of matter or an event in the history of mind.

Let's start with a syllogism.

Major premise: Thoughts are part of you, or an act of you, or a dimension of you. You do not belong to your thoughts; they belong to you. They are your thoughts. Perhaps they also exist outside of you, perhaps not, but they exist as part of you. They are only one part of you. There are many other parts of you too: body parts and soul parts such as feelings and desires and willing and choosing and proving. None of these are material things in space that can be measured mathematically, as matter can, but they are nonmaterial things, events that really happen in your mind.

Minor premise: You are a tiny part of the universe. Perhaps you are also more than the universe, but you are part of the universe. That's where you are: "You are here." I didn't say that just your body is here but that you are here, you, this person who thinks—you are here now, in this room in this city, now. That's where these thoughts are occurring. Not in Heaven or Hell or Purgatory or wherever angels live, but here on earth.

By the way, I think you are indeed more than a part of the universe, because you can know some universal truths about the whole universe, and in order to know the whole of anything, the subject that's doing the thinking can't be merely part of the object thought about. The light that lights up things cannot be merely one of the things lit up. Action and reception are different. Understanding is not merely being understood. The subject is not just an object.

But you don't need to understand that "by the way" point or agree with that to follow my argument.

From my two premises, that thoughts are parts of you and that you are part of the universe, it follows that (in some sense) thoughts are part of the universe. They happen here and now even though they are not simply material things made of molecules that take up space.

What is the universe? It is, or includes, all the matter, time, and space that exists. And matter, time, and space are all relative to each other. So are matter and energy. And, apparently, so are material energy and spiritual energy, like body and soul, or body and mind, or body and spirit.

We know that the universe came from a singular event that science calls the Big Bang and theists call the act of creation.

Let's think about that event with basic scientific reasoning. The basic principle of all reasoning, especially scientific reasoning, is the principle of causality. Nothing just happens without an adequate, sufficient cause. Nothing happens without a reason. Perhaps we do not know the reason, perhaps there are even some things whose reasons for happening we *cannot* know, but there must be some kind of reason for everything. If a large blue rabbit suddenly appeared on my head, no one would say, "Oh, well, rabbits just happen."

Stephen Hawking was called the most intelligent scientist in the world. He once answered the question "How can there be a Big Bang without a Big Banger?" by saying that "universes just happen." So the most intelligent scientist in the world abandoned the single most fundamental principle of all science. Why? Obviously to avoid something like a Creator. And probably for personal reasons: he probably equated a Creator with the God of the Bible, and he equated the God of the Bible with a kind of cosmic Puritan tyrant who arbitrarily decided to spoil our fun whenever he could. Perhaps he thought that any trustable God couldn't have let him live with his tragic paralyzing disease. I think we have to sympathize with him there, even if we disagree. There does seem to be a lot of evidence against God, a lot of evil that we cannot explain.

But even if it's not obviously irrational to deny that a Creator-God exists, it is obviously irrational to deny that all events need causes. Everything that begins has to have a cause that is adequate to account for why it began.

But then that must be true of the universe too, because the universe began, about 13.7 billion years ago. If you don't like the word "God," then use some other word, such as "x" or "Steven Spielberg." But something has to be the first cause, the cause of the first event. Events, changes, do not go back to infinity; they go back only to the Big Bang, 13.7 billion years ago. All of them do.

Thoughts are events. They are mental events. All events need causes. Therefore, mental events also need causes.

The *content* of a thought or the *meaning* of a thought or the *truth* of a thought does not need a cause. The number two does not need a cause, nor does the fact that two plus two is four. Truth does not need a cause. Those things are not events, with beginnings. They are timeless.

But the fact that an idea appears to a mind is an event. It happens. It has a beginning. So it needs a cause. What is that cause?

The first and most obvious answer to that question is that the immediate cause of your thoughts is you, your mind, or the power of your mind, just as the cause of the food you eat is the earth, and the power of the earth to make plants and animals live.

Thoughts are acts of your mind just as burps are acts of your digestive system. Materialists think that the mind is only the brain, and thoughts are just brain burps. That's not only insulting but also stupid. The brain is only one of your organs. It is "a computer made of meat." Computers don't think. The people who design and program and use computers think, just as the people who write and read books think. But books don't think. If you say computers think, you must say that an abacus thinks a little bit, because it's a little computer. If you added some batteries and springs to the abacus to make it a clumsy handheld adding machine, would that mean that it could think? Of course not. Now add a lot more of the same kind of stuff to make it a supercomputer as big as Rhode Island. Does that mean it can think? No. Thinking is a different *kind* of thing from atoms in space. If a hundred atoms can't think, neither can a hundred trillion atoms.

So, the immediate cause of your thoughts is your mind, as the immediate cause of your burps is your body. But both your mind and body, in turn, have causes. And that complex chain of causes goes back, through evolution, to the Big Bang, and thus the Big Banger.

We have some control over our bodies, so we must be more than just bodies. We can choose to burp or not, and we can choose to think or not, and we can choose to suppress a burp, and we can choose to suppress a thought. So, there is free will among that complex chain of causes that produces both physical events such as burping and spiritual events such as thinking. That does not mean that those free choices are uncaused, that they are millions of little eternal creator-gods with no cause and no beginning.

Thoughts come from somewhere. Everything that begins has a cause of its beginning.

Why isn't it as obvious to most of us that there must a First Cause of all mental events just as there must be a First Cause of all physical events? Because we can easily detect the intermediate physical causes by our science, and we can stop at these as the scientifically adequate explanation. Science does not need to raise the more important question, the philosophical question, the question of the ultimate cause. But human nature does raise it, because human nature is curious about much more than science can detect.

And since mind and body are united, we can detect the biological causes and conditions of our thoughts too, by our sciences of physiology and cybernetics and psychology. But that does not eliminate God any more than the discovery of the stomach eliminates God when explaining our burps. The pathways by which God feeds both body and mind are long and complex and extend back to the Big Bang. The very existence of the totality of the things that science explains is not explained by science. It is taken for granted.

So there has to be a first, uncaused cause of the whole universe. And since the universe is the sum total of all time and space and matter, that cause cannot be just one of the things in time and space and matter. It must be more than time and space and matter. It must be eternal and immaterial and mental, not physical.

Once you see that, the temptation is to make this First Cause (or God, if you're not allergic to the G-word) into the immediate cause of everything, and not give any power or credit to secondary causes, or caused causes, dependent causes, either physical or mental. But the First Cause established an order of second causes. God didn't micromanage everything, so you shouldn't either. The Hindu *Upanishads* succumbs to that temptation by calling Brahman, their name for the supreme God, "the thinker of every thought." So, the human self disappears into the divine self. And mainline Islam, the Ash'arite school of Muslim philosophy, which has been the main line in Muslim philosophy since the eighth or ninth century A.D., does that too in the material order by calling Allah the immediate cause of everything, without any created intermediaries having any independent power to be anything but occasions for God's actions. (This is technically called *occasionalism* in philosophy.)

To bring this long answer to a quick end, the primary cause of every event must be the First Cause, or God, but there are also secondary causes. Your body, and all its actions, as part of the universe, can be traced back to the Big Bang and the Big Banger, but it is also dependent on many secondary causes, including your parents making love and your whole ancestral family history and the history of evolution. Since your thinking is also part of you and you are part of the universe, it is also part of the universe, part of time, and that too must be traced back to the Creator, but also through many intermediaries, including your teachers and your parents and your ancestors.

Your mind and your body are not two separate things but two powers or dimensions of the one thing you call *you*. So, they always go together, like the words and the meaning of a book. Materialism reduces all meaning to words, and spiritualism, or "spirituality" (a very suspicious word), reduces all words to meanings, reduces matter to spirit.

The practical point or payoff of this is that you have to use the same reasoning for your mind as for your body. If there is a God, you have to thank Him for your mental food as well as your physical food. You thank Him for your bodily food even though you yourself may have planted and watered and harvested and prepared and eaten that food, because He is the First Cause of the whole process. I think the same applies to your ideas, or your mental food. Thank God for every good idea you ever had, even that one, whether God gave it to you through all those intermediaries or whether He did it though His angels or whether He did it directly through inspiration. He can work in all three ways.

So, if you believe that, then before thinking, as well as before eating, you should pray, "Bless us, O Lord, and these Thy gifts which we are about to receive from Thy bounty."

I think that the instinct of gratitude, the instinct to say "thank you," is the deep psychological origin of all religion. In our spiritual geography the right latitude is the attitude of gratitude. That's the corollary or payoff or "bottom line" practically of all this theoretical analysis. And I am more certain I am right about the practical corollary than I am about the theoretical analysis.

Can you tell us a piece of wisdom from your father?

Sure. When I was about twelve, I lusted after the latest Lionel train set, a bright yellow Union Pacific diesel passenger train. For a month before Christmas, I kept pestering my father about it.

One day, he sat me down and said, "Do you know why we celebrate Christmas?" I thought that I had better pass this exam if I wanted the reward, so I said, "Sure. It's Jesus' birthday." "So why do we give each other gifts on Christmas?" "Because God gave us Jesus as His gift to us." "Good. And why did God do that?" "To save us." "And why did God want to save us?" "Because He loves us." "Good. So why do we give each other gifts?" "Because we love each other." "Very good. Now I know how much you want that Lionel train for Christmas, but it's very expensive, and I'm not very rich, so I might not be able to afford to buy it for you. If I can't, will you still know how much I love you?"

Oh, oh, I thought. A trick question. Which answer is most likely to get me the train? Can I bribe him to give me the train if I say I won't believe he loves me if he doesn't? Or should I give him the answer he wants to hear? He's smarter than me. I can't outsmart him. I guess when everything else fails, I'd better fall back on honesty. "I know you love me, Dad, even if you can't afford the train."

"Thanks, son. You just gave me a great Christmas present."

He was happy, but I wasn't. "Darn it, I let him get away. Now he doesn't have to buy me the train."

Well, I got the train. I still have it. But it's not working anymore; it's rusting away in the attic.

But the lesson isn't rusting away in the attic of my brain. It's still working.

I heard somebody define a liberal as someone who doesn't believe in evil and a conservative as someone who doesn't believe in goodness. Which do you think is more dangerous: optimism or pessimism? Naivete or cynicism and suspicion?

Well, first of all, I don't think either a liberal or a conservative would accept your description of them. Most liberals believe that evil does exist, and most conservatives believe that goodness does exist, in the very same place: in conservatives. Machiavelli says trust nobody. So don't trust him, especially when he tells you to trust nobody. Rousseau says trust everybody. We're all immaculate conceptions. Fine. So trust his critics, like me.

Cynics say "guilty till proven innocent," and naive people say, "innocent until proven guilty." I think they're both right but in opposite areas of life. A fundamental principle of science is to treat every idea as false until proven true, and a fundamental principle of our law is that people should be treated as innocent until proven guilty. So I think we should be more critical of ideas and less of people, more intolerant of sins and more tolerant of sinners.

But to do that, you have to distinguish the two. There are too many people who say, "If you hate my idea, you hate me, and if you love me, you must love my ideas." An idea can be true even if the person who holds it is wicked and full of hate. If we discovered that Einstein was a Nazi spy who loved Hitler and was planning to give him the atom bomb so he could conquer the world, that would not prove that E does not equal MC squared. And an idea can be false even if the person who holds it is good and lovable. Jimmy Carter was a much better person than Richard Nixon, but his economic ideas were a disaster, and Nixon's were a success.

Hard-hearted people treat people like hypotheses — guilty until proven innocent. That's a guaranteed conversation killer. "It's raining." "Oh yeah? Prove it." Soft-minded people treat hypotheses like people — innocent until proven guilty. Advertisers love those people.

Outside of advertising and science, even ideas should be treated as innocent until proven guilty. That's what Socrates did. He eventually found a lot of those ideas guilty (false), but only after carefully listening to them. He knew that you can't be good at playing any kind of music, including the music of philosophical wisdom, unless you first listen.

God could have given us two mouths and one ear, but instead He gave us two ears and one mouth, so that we could listen twice as much as we speak.

I've wandered pretty far from your question, haven't I?

Well, let me say one thing about liberals and conservatives, or Democrats and Republicans. The Devil doesn't care whether you worship the donkey or the elephant as long as you don't worship God. For many of us, politics is our religion.

We're religious about politics — it's our absolute, our passion — and political about religion — we use religion as a means to political ends.

You've been criticized as "simplistic." How do you respond to that?

I say that I don't deserve that compliment.

Kierkegaard wrote a book with the title *Purity of Heart Is to Will One Thing.* He invented some really great titles.

The most important things are the simplest things: being, truth, goodness, beauty, love, persons, and above all, God. These are all simple things. God is the simplest of all: there are no divisions in Him, not even between His justice and His mercy, or even between Him and His attributes. He's not just someone who is just and merciful; He *is* justice and He *is* mercy.

And the distinction between the three Persons of the Trinity is not a division, because the three Persons are more perfectly united by love than any one of them is by mere quantitative oneness.

That's true of human love too: love unites you more deeply with the beloved than you are united to yourself, because you will give up yourself for the one you love, but you will not give up that one for yourself. If you really love someone, you are more concerned for his happiness than for your own, and you are more threatened by his death than by your own. So, the Trinitarian God is more perfectly one and simple than the Unitarian God.

The most important things are always the simplest things. There are also complex things that are important—for instance, super-computers, the subatomic structure of the universe, the genetic code, and the Library of Congress. But none of them is nearly as important as the things I mentioned: love, joy, beauty, and so forth.

First things are simple. God is *the* First Thing; therefore, the first in simplicity. The first thing you were was a single cell, a human zygote. The first thing that ever happened to you was that you were conceived, you were procreated, you were brought into being. The first step of any journey is the most important, because all subsequent steps depend on it. "One foot up and one foot down: that's the way to London Town." The ancient Greeks said: "Well begun is half done."

One of the simplest words in our language is the word "I."

It's the shortest word in the language and the skinniest letter in the alphabet. You are one you, one person, but you have many attributes, and you do many things, and you know many things, and you experience many things, but it's all the same simple "I" that is them and has them and does them and knows them and experiences them.

Your soul is more important than your body, and it's also simpler than your body. It's not made of atoms, and you can't cut it up into parts as you can a body. You can't have half a soul. You can only have a bad soul, or a weak soul, or a stupid soul. You don't make your soul any fatter when you eat or skinnier when you diet. You don't lose any of your soul when you get a haircut.

"Simple" does not necessarily mean "not mysterious." God is both the simplest and the most mysterious being. Your soul is more mysterious than your body, even though it's also simpler.

Your soul owns your body; your body does not own your soul. Your body is part of you too—in fact, part of your essence, your essential nature; but only your soul can think and say "I." It makes you a person. A corpse is no longer a person; it's a body without a soul. A ghost is a person, even though it's a soul without a body. It's an incomplete person, because its soul is meant to be the soul of a body, unlike an angel, which is complete as a spirit alone. So, you are a complete human person again after death only after the resurrection of the body.

One person can own many things, but no one can own a person. That's why slavery is a lie. It treats a person as a thing, as merely one of many things.

How to get to Mars is complex, but how to get to Heaven is simple. "Trust and obey" won't get you to Mars, but it is simple. And supercomputers are complex, but they won't get you to Heaven.

How to understand people is simple: love them. I said "simple," not "easy." "Simple" doesn't mean "easy."

Past time and future time are complex, but the present moment is simple. And it's also the most important, because the past is dead, and the future is not yet born.

But "simple" doesn't mean "easy." It's easy to live in the past. Regret is easy. It's easy to live in the future. Fear is easy. It's hard to live in the present. But it's the only time that's real. Squirm as you will, you can never escape it.

Love is present. Nostalgia is not love, because its object is past. Desire is not love, because its object is future. Love is always in the present moment, and it is present to the other, and it presents itself as a gift, a present, to the other. Notice the unity among those three meanings of the word "present"—not past or future, not absent, and not withheld.

Is that philosophy too simple for you?

Thanks for the compliment.

That's not simple. That's very
philosophical. Can you give us some
really simple, practical advice?

OK. How's this? Here are some Nevers:

Never go to the deep woods without mosquito repellent.

Never take the queen's knight's pawn with your queen.

Never cheat, even on yourself.

Never stop loving.

Never stop hoping.

Never stop believing.

Never forget to smell the roses every day. Literally. (Why is that so hard?)

Never prefer being divorced in Hawaii to being in love in the Bronx.

Never stop smiling at least once every hour.

Oh, and here's one more concrete thing: learn from your feet. God gave you two of them, so in order to go anywhere, you have to have one foot up and one foot down, one foot in the air and one on the ground. If you keep both feet on the ground, you never go anywhere; you just stand there. If you keep both feet in the air, you are either upside down or levitating. It's a natural symbol for living in both worlds, is and ought, realism and idealism. Chesterton says that we are not moles burrowing in the earth, nor are we balloons flying off into the sky, but we are trees, with our roots planted on the earth and our branches reaching out into the heavens.

You can also learn a lot from your knees, but only if you bend them.

God

Why do you have to bring God into everything?[1]

I don't.

He's already there.

He is the only one no one can ever "bring into" anything because He's in everything, as Shakespeare is in every syllable in *Hamlet*. Does it make any sense to ask, "Why do you have to bring Shakespeare into everything in *Hamlet*?"

If He's not in everything, He's not in anything; He's only a myth like Zeus or Santa Claus.

As Shakespeare writes the story of *Hamlet*, God writes the story of you. The rest of the universe is only the setting for that story. The setting is to be explained by the characters. Materialism is the strange superstition that the characters are to be explained by the setting. Atheist humanism is inhuman.

But I think I sense the point behind your question. I'm at least as annoyed as you are by fundamentalists who import God and the Bible into everything artificially, like the fans at baseball games who hold up signs with "John 3:16" on them. They make embarrassingly bad religious movies and write even worse

[1] This is a question that was asked of me not in a public Q & A but in a private conversation, especially about my books.

33

religious novels (Tim LaHaye and Frank Peretti write some of the worst novels I have ever tried to read), and emote passionately about stupid, silly, sappy, sloppy, shallow little "praise choruses" and "Christian rock," which is an insult to rock as well as to Christianity. I dated a girl once who insisted on praying before every kiss. As I said, I dated her *once*.

Contrast this with the heart of Jesuit spirituality, which is "finding God everywhere," but naturally and mostly unconsciously. And Dominican spirituality, which applies the basic principle of Thomistic metaphysics, that God the Creator gives the act of existence to everything at every moment. God is being itself, existence itself, not limited by any finite essence; and existence is at the heart of everything and makes actual its essence, its properties, its accidents, its relationships—everything.

Conclusion: God is at the heart of everything, necessarily and by nature. You don't have to import Him like an alien.

What is your favorite proof for the existence of God?

Jesus.

Jesus is the best proof.

If God does not exist, Jesus is the biggest fool who ever lived. If you can believe that, you can believe that Stalin and Hitler were saints.

My second favorite proof for God's existence is the music of Johann Sebastian Bach. I know three ex-atheists or ex-agnostics who told me that they were converted by the *St. Matthew Passion*. One is a monk and two are philosophers — very wise ones.

Most philosophers today are what they call "analytic philosophers." They emphasize the left-brain hemisphere: analytic, quantitative, digital, binary, computer logic. That's fine, but we also have a right hemisphere, which does intuition and understanding and empathy and analogy, seeing "big pictures" and appreciating things whose truth and profundity are hard to put into words—things such as beauty and love and music. To understand the Bach proof, you must use that power of the mind, which is increasingly neglected in our culture of video games and the Internet and technology.

The oldest evidence of the presence of humans present is the wonderfully realistic and alive thirty-thousand-year-old paintings in the Lascaux caves in France. "Art is the signature of humanity." They didn't invent primitive computers; they invented primitive art. The abacus came long after calligraphy.

Religion doesn't begin with logical proofs for the existence of God. In the infancy of humanity, and of the individual, you "just know" that there are simply some things that you "can't not know." Some sort of God, some sort of greater-than-us Being, is one of those things. About 99 percent of humans who have lived before the invention of the Internet have believed that. If they are wrong, then they are adults who are still playing and living by the game typical of a three-year-old, playing with an invisible friend that they have invented. They are, quite literally, insane. Freud is honest enough to draw that logical conclusion. I don't have the chutzpah or the arrogance to pin the label of insanity on any of my fellow humans, including the greatest minds in history, not only in philosophy but also in science, including Pythagoras, Aristotle, Copernicus, Kepler, Descartes, Pascal, Galileo, Newton, and Einstein.

So that's my third favorite proof. It's not a proof, just a very strong probability: that our parents, our ancestors, our great teachers are more likely to be right than their teenage children.

My fourth favorite proof is from the existential consequences of atheism. It's the loss of hope. We all innately hope there is a perfect Being and a perfect Heaven. We all have a lover's quarrel with the world. We all have Augustine's restless heart. If there is no rest for that quest, if there is no better world than this and no better beings than us, we have to give up our deepest hope and our deepest desire. That's a big price. In fact, that's the sign over the entrance to Hell: "Abandon hope, ye who enter here." So I guess my fourth favorite proof is Pascal's wager: religious faith may be a wager, a bet, a hope rather than a proof and a certainty, but it's the world's best bet because making that bet is your only chance of winning, and not making it is a guaranteed loss.

And then there are also a few dozen very good purely logical arguments, such as the moral argument (what gives moral conscience its authority?) and the cosmological argument (how can there be a Big Bang without a Big Banger?).

Does God have a sense of humor?

The question itself is hilarious.

Yes.

God laughs.

At us.

We are His great joke.

Not to laugh at God's great joke is to be really, really stupid.

God wants to fill our mouth with laughter (Job 8:21), but we want to fill our mouth with arguments (Job 23:4).

"Out of the mouths of babes and sucklings He has ordained strength and praise" (see Matt. 21:16, Douay-Rheims). Before they can speak, babies recognize happiness in a smile. (They are wiser than the "experts" in the Global Happiness Project who designated the five Scandinavian countries the happiest, and five African countries the unhappiest, in the world. Everyone speaks of "those dour Africans" and "those smiling Scandinavians," of course! And, of course, the suicide rates have nothing to do with happiness.)

The same wisdom in babies that recognizes happiness, also recognizes what is funny. Babies laugh, just at life, even when they are not being tickled. Later, when they learn words, they laugh at all the words for "laughter": titter, twitter, snicker, giggle, guffaw, and the words for the laughers and the laughed at: goof-off, goofus, doofus.

The nearly universal word for laughter is *Ha Ha Ha* or *Ho Ho Ho* or sometimes *Hee Hee Hee*. The H sound is the aspirant, the sound of breathing. To breathe is to laugh. Life itself is its own greatest joke. To exhale is to excrete used-up air.

God promised blessings to the whole world through Sarah, Abraham's postmenopausal wife, and when He promised that to Abraham, he "fell on his face and laughed," for Sarah was ninety. It was the world's first great Jewish joke.

God also chose the name of the miraculous promise child, Isaac, which means "he laughs."

Kids with cancer who laugh at Ronald McDonald clowns recover faster. (See Raymond Moody on the healing power of laughter.)

This could not be unless laughter put us in contact with God, the source of life.

AIDS kills you by killing off T cells, which fight disease. Laughing restores and multiplies T cells.

Is that healing power of laughter something of mind or body, spiritual or physical? The question is meaningful to us but not to God. When God works on us, He works on both body and soul (because He works on us as we are, and we are both body and soul, always, until death), just as when an author writes, he writes both words and meanings, and when a musician composes, he composes both sounds and relationships among sounds (melodies, harmonies).

Chesterton says that Jesus was completely human, unlike all pagan heroes, who suppressed something: tears, fears, anger, pain, *something* human. So where, then, was Jesus' laughter? He must have had the world's best sense of humor if He had the world's best and completest human nature. The answer, Chesterton says, is in His prayer. When He got closest to His Father, when He went up into a mountain alone to pray, He had to hide something from His disciples, something that was just too big for them to endure. Chesterton says it was His laughter.

It was human laughter, but it was also divine laughter. That's why it was too big for us to endure.

Anyone who says God has no sense of humor has never stared at an ostrich. Anyone who says God has no sense of humor has never looked into a mirror.

Jesus used a jackass for His most important journey, into Jerusalem to save the world. He still has the same weird taste in animals: He uses *us*.

Prayer and Meditation

What is your favorite method of prayer?

To "pray without ceasing," as St. Paul tells us (1 Thess. 5:17). To blend prayer with everything else. To make work a prayer. To overcome the separation between religion and life, the unfortunate idea we all have that "religion" is something different from life, something "pious" or "for religious people" or only for special times and places; something that ordinary sinners and cynics and selfish people dismiss as sissified and embarrassing.

The only way to do that — to overcome that superstition — is with prayers that are unconscious rather than conscious, because it's not psychologically possible to concentrate on praying while you are concentrating on solving math problems or catching a wave or swatting a fly. And when the prayers are conscious, and verbal, make them very short but frequent — such as "Yes, Lord" or *"Fiat"* or *"Ad te, Domine"* (offering it up). Or even a gesture: the Sign of the Cross if you are alone, or a salute (to help you remember who your Commanding Officer is) that does not look like a salute, and thus is not intrusive. Your Morning Offering (of *all* your prayers, works, joys, and sufferings) establishes this; frequent reminders simply frequently remind you of it. You don't have to be very pious or holy or contemplative or "religious" just to touch your forehead.

My second answer is praying Scripture, reading the Bible as prayer, conversing with God about it. It's His love letter to you, after all. Like almost everybody else, my favorite Scriptures for prayer are the psalms, the prayer book God Himself gave us and the one Jesus and His disciples used, the one Jews have used for three thousand years. The more you pray them, the more you see in them, even the ones that seem at first hard and polemical and even self-righteous. God put them there for us to use. Just remember who your real "enemies" are: your own sins, and the evil spirits who tempt you.

My third answer is the Rosary, John Paul II's favorite prayer, too. It has power.

Our main problem is time: we resist giving time to God. So I take a five-minute hourglass, and I turn it upside down, and I pretend that the next five minutes is the only time I will have because I will die in five minutes. What do I say to God?

I tried setting a watch alarm to go off at 3:00 p.m. every day to remind me to take this holiest of all times, the time Christ died, to pray for a minute. But that didn't work because I have ADD and I forgot to set it, and I didn't hear it, and I goofed up setting it (I'm capable of messing up even the simplest mechanical device), and I eventually lost the watch. I tried to do it without an alarm but failed miserably.

Oh, and find some other prayer time besides first thing in the morning and last thing at night (though they should be your first brief thought of God and your last), because those are the two times when there are the most sleepy cobwebs in your brain. Give God a set amount of time every day. Start with something realistic and doable, such as five minutes, or even one; more is better than less, but something is better than nothing.

When, where, and how are not as important as *just doing it*.

Do you recommend meditation exercises?

Yes.

Very highly.

Everyone should take at least fifteen minutes a day to practice what some call "mindfulness" and others call "the relaxation response" (the title of Dr. Herbert Benson's book). It has immediate physical and chemical effects that last all day—in fact, last a lifetime if you keep at it—in making you calmer, happier, and more peaceful and at the same time more alert, aware, and awake (more alpha waves, fewer beta and theta waves).

Everyone who has done this testifies that it works—that it is an eminently practical investment of time. The only problem is that you have to do it, not just think about doing it.

So why don't we do it consistently?

Why don't I?

For the same reason we're not saints.

Experience teaches us that genuinely, honestly unselfish love is the way to deepest joy, yet we don't do it. The holier we are, the happier we are; and the more egotistically babyish we are, the unhappier we are. Yet we repeatedly choose self-centered babyness over unselfconscious love. It's because we are brain damaged. We are, in fact, insane. That's what "original sin" means. Einstein defined "insanity" as doing the same stupid thing over and over again and expecting a better result the next time.

Our only hope is that our Father dearly loves his severely brain-damaged children.

What methods do you recommend for prayer and meditation?

Method is only 1 percent of the solution; 99 percent is to do it, to start, whichever method you use.

This is essential: just do it.

Here is a simple, nonthreatening, no-risk path to health and happiness, an open door right in front of us, and we turn away from it because we say we don't have the time for it. We are slaves to time, or rather to false time, to clock time, to our schedule time.

But if you give God even a little bit of the loaves and fishes of your time, He will miraculously multiply them, and at the end of the day, you will feel that you have accomplished surprisingly much. On the other hand, if you grasp your loaves and fishes to yourself, they will not taste all that good, or they will rot, or they will diminish. It works that way every time.

But in order to "stop and smell the roses," you first have to stop doing the stuff you are doing, whatever it is. Ask yourself honestly and sanely (even insane people have a well of sanity in them):

How important is that stuff?

Are you God?

Will the universe cease to exist if you take your hands off it for fifteen minutes?

My favorite sermon of all time is the shortest one I ever heard. (I have ADD and get bored very quickly.) God preached it to St. Catherine. He said, in effect, "I will now sum up all of divine revelation in four words, in just two two-word sentences. Here is everything I have been trying to get across to you every moment of your life and in every page in the Bible: *I'm God; you're not.*"

The reason we have to keep returning to meditation is that we keep forgetting both parts of that sermon.

But you didn't answer my question. Granted
that method is not the first thing, we do use
some method. So what is it? How do you
meditate? We have a lot of prayers—the
psalms and the Lord's Prayer and the
Rosary—but what about meditation?

Fair enough. I will answer your question.

First, set aside fifteen minutes as sacred time. Don't let anything interrupt you that's less important than the house catching
on fire or Grandma falling out the window.

Next, after time, comes place. Find a quiet place and sit in a
comfortable chair. Not *too* comfortable, though.

Simple books such as Dr. Gregory Bottaro's *The Mindful
Catholic* and Dr. Herbert Benson's *The Relaxation Response* are
good. Probably much better than what I'm going to tell you. But
I'll tell you ten little exercises to give your mind more power
and peace.

Do one each day, for ten days, in the order that is given.
They move from the more concrete to the more abstract, because for us, who are not pure spirits, the abstract depends on
the concrete.

After giving all ten a fair chance, repeat for another ten days the one or two that work best for you. Don't give up on any one that you have chosen, no matter how much you are tempted to do so, until fifteen minutes have passed. This will feel impossible at first, but you will learn to persist and succeed. It's not rocket science or brain surgery. Millions do it.

1. Concentrate on how each part of your body feels, starting with your left big toe. Feel every finger, without touching anything. Learn to distinguish your toes. Get acquainted with your belly button, your earlobes, your shoulder blades. Go slow, don't rush.

2. Concentrate on each thing you see. Notice as many details as you can.

3. Concentrate on all the sounds you hear, one by one. There are far more than you think, especially if you are outdoors.

4. Meet your memory and imagination. Conjure up, in detail, sights and sounds you saw and heard yesterday, or fifty years ago, and how they made you feel.

5. Conjure up fictional sights and sounds, in detail. You might try St. Ignatius's "composition of place" from the *Spiritual Exercises*.[2]

6. Meet all the little pleasures and pains in your body at this moment. Again, go through each part as you did in exercise 1, this time feeling pleasure or pain in each one. Cause yourself slight pains; for instance, by

[2] Composition of place involves using all of one's senses to place oneself in the scene one is meditating on, such as a scene from the Gospel.

pressing your fingers hard against a wall. Just be aware of it. Don't hate it *or* love it.

7. Meet your soul, which gives life to your body. Meet the *life* of each body part that you felt in exercise 1, and of your body as a whole. Feel the difference between your body seen as a corpse, an object, and your body felt as you, the live subject.

8. Become aware of your awareness of each body part. You cannot see it or hear it or measure it as you can feel the parts of your body, yet you cannot deny it. It is the energy that lets you feel each part.

9. Become aware of the existence of a single "you" that you call "I" or "myself" that possesses all these body parts and all these mental powers and does all these exercises. And more: become aware of your mental power to know some certain, undoubtable, unchangeable, eternal truths, such as the truths of mathematics and the fundamental principles of ethics such as the Golden Rule. Think about your thinking about this, not to prove anything but just to be aware of your awareness of it. Don't try to imagine it; awareness is not physical; therefore, it's not imaginable. It has no shape or color or size. But you can know it anyway. Use it. Exercise it. Feel the truth and certainty that $2 + 2 = 4$. Rejoice in it. Thank God for it.

10. Become aware of your power to become aware that there is an Omniscient and Omnipotent Being who created and designed each of these parts and mental powers for you. Do nothing but direct your attention and awareness to Him. He is right there where you are, not far away; present, not absent. Accept His

existence and His presence and His total knowledge of you and His total love of you. You don't have to do anything about it right now; just be aware of it. This is not a test, that you can fail. It is a fact, like yourself.

What about us busy people who don't have time for meditation?

You don't have enough time to save time?

To turn time from tyrant to friend?

The most common excuse for not taking time to do meditation is that you do not have the time.

In other words, you do not live as if you disposed of your time as you dispose of your money, but as if time disposed of you as a master disposes of his slaves. Your master does not give you enough time. You only have twenty-four hours each day; if you had twenty-four and a quarter hours, you could do this, but you don't; therefore, you can't. It is, of course, a silly, stupid lie.

Why do you believe such a lie? Because you are probably an addict, like most people in our civilization: an addict to the flywheel of work, of efficiency, of time management. Ironically, in focusing such attention on time management, we who serve the clock as our slave driver are far worse at time management than our ancestors, who didn't care that much about it, who did not live as much by the clock.

What is the most obvious difference between their world and ours? Technology. The result of our immense progress in technology has been that no one seems to have any leisure, any free time anymore. But all of technology is a series of time-saving devices! Where did all the time go? To Iowa?

Time is like money. There are many opportunities to invest it and make more. This is one of them. Taking time for exercises such as the ten in my last answer is taking time back from your slave master. It gives you more time, not less. It generates time interest on the time capital that you invest.

Time can multiply, like the loaves and fishes that the little boy in John's Gospel gave to Jesus so that He could feed five thousand people with them. If we do not give up time, it will not be multiplied, just as, if we do not give up some money for an investment, it will not be multiplied.

This works on the supernatural level, of course. The loaves and fishes signify time for prayer. It even works on the natural level: you might not explicitly give your time to God in prayer, but He accepts it anyway, and multiplies it, because He is the one who designed human nature to do this kind of thing and to profit by it.

The clock is certainly the most life-changing machine ever invented. It has given us a radically new and radically unnatural meaning to time, and therefore to life, for your life is your "life-time." (That's why your gift of time to your family is so precious: it is the gift of your life.) Time has been lifted out of nature, including our own human nature, and made into an independent entity, like a god. Time used to be measured by meaning, by man, by soul, by spirit. Its name was *kairos*, which meant "time for" something. But we think of time as *chronos*, which is measured by matter, by clocks, and by the impersonal movements of the heavenly bodies through the sky, or of the decay of radioactive particles.

What about us busy people who don't have time for meditation?

Learn that there is a time that is not measurable by clocks. Live in *kairos*. Make *chronos* your servant, not your master.

Why does everyone have less time today than ever before? Because we have more time-saving devices than ever before. That is neither a joke nor a self-contradiction; it is a fact. The obvious difference between life today and life yesterday is the immense expansion of technology. But all of technology is a series of time-saving devices, from fireplaces to microwave ovens, from chariots to airliners, from the telegraph to the smartphone, from the library to the Internet. And the more of these time-saving devices we have, the less free time we have. Our parents had more time than we do, and our grandparents even more. Why? Because they had less technology.

The obvious cause of this paradox is that we have become addicts, slaves to our slaves. Our slaves are made of computer chips and plastic and steel. They are more efficient, as well as more morally innocent, than flesh-and-blood slaves. But they serve the same purpose.

Now, suppose you owned two slaves and you got twenty more. They do more work for you, of course, but do they give you more time? No, less, because you have to supervise them and provide for them. That truth did not change when machines replaced people as our slaves.

Break free!

Emancipate yourself!

We need another emancipation proclamation.

We don't have to throw away our devices, just our enslavement to them. The first Emancipation Proclamation did not require the murder of the slave owners, just freedom from them.

I am not saying we need to turn back the clock on technology (although most people enjoy doing that for a while, while on vacation), but on our attitude toward it. That is indeed a turning back of the clock. As G. K. Chesterton pointed out, "You can't turn back the clock" is a simple, stupid lie.

You can.

The clock is a human invention, and when it keeps bad time, you can indeed turn it back. Nothing prevents us from exchanging a car for a bicycle, or fast food for home-grown food, or an unsatisfying job in the fast lane for a satisfying job in the slow lane. Nothing but that silly superstition.

There's a connection between being enslaved to time, to technology, and to excuses. When you start giving excuses, that's usually the time to start doing what you're inventing excuses for not doing. The easiest excuse is "tomorrow."

How did that work for Macbeth? For Alice? She asked for jam, and the Red Queen replied, "There's jam tomorrow"—but tomorrow is never today. "Tomorrow is always a day away." America's best philosopher is an orange-haired teenage fictional girl named Annie.

You will never "find" the time to do it. You have to make the time to do it. And you can do that, because time is your servant, not your master. It's like your food: you eat it; it does not eat you. It's like money: you can spend it on anything you want. What you spend it on reveals what's in your heart— what you love the most.

Don't live by the clock and use people; live by people (including yourself) and use the clock.

Don't reverse masters and slaves, ends and means. Time is a horse. Ride it; don't let it ride you. Manage it; don't let it manage you.

You can use it for bad or selfish ends, or you can use it for good and loving ends, or you can let it use you. Only one of those three lifestyles makes any sense.

Religion

What do you think is the origin of religion?

It's got to be a universal instinct, because religion is universal. Even atheists usually begin by being religious.

Some say it's fear.

I say it's gratitude.

Maybe fear is the origin of bad religion, unhappy religion, but gratitude is the origin of good religion, joyful religion. People become atheists as a reaction against unhappy religion, not joyful religion.

Gratitude is a primal instinct because we know that we are recipients. We are given millions of good things as gifts throughout life — things we did not plan or work for — but first of all, we are given life itself as a gift that we did not plan or work for or deserve. How could we deserve to be given it if we did not even exist before we had it?

You can say it was your parents, not God, who gave you that gift; but "piety," *pietas,* in ancient languages always means gratitude and honor to both God (or gods) and parents (and ancestors, extended parents). That's why atheists almost always lose respect and honor for their parents and ancestors at the same time they lose it for God. And that's why religion and family always flourish or decline together, both in history and in personal lifestyle. Religion leads you to have more children, and having children makes you more religious. Statistics prove that these two truths are not mere social, changeable stereotypes.

People believe many religions and many alternatives to religion. But atheists, agnostics, humanists, transhumanists, Marxists, Buddhists, Taoists, Confucians, Hindus, Jews, Christians, Muslims, Republicans, and even Democrats all have human nature, and therefore all have the capacity for (and not just the capacity for but the natural tendency toward) a cosmic, universal gratitude, a gratitude for everything good.

And good is everywhere. Everything has to have some good; evil cannot exist except as a parasite on a good, the perversion of a good. What do belly button lint, Jersey mosquitoes, lawyers, politicians, White Castle hamburgers, hemorrhoids, Studebakers, insurance agents, baby burps, and mimes have in common? They all contain hidden beauty.

The worst moment in the life of an atheist is not deep sorrow but deep joy and gratitude—gratitude for life, for existence, for everything —but for an atheist, there is no one to thank for that. It just happens.

The atheist has then only three choices:

1. To suppress the gratitude, to call it a fake and an illusion (and that will turn him into a bitter cynic)
2. To say that this gratitude is wise and good, even though there is no God to be grateful to—and that will turn him into a Camus, who, like his protagonist Dr. Rieux in *The Plague*, believed three logically incompatible things: that there is no God, that you can't be a saint without God, and that the meaning of life is to be a saint (full of love and gratitude)

3. To reason that since part of being a saint is to feel that gratitude, therefore, to follow that pointing finger of gratitude is to move out of yourself to something like God

Why are there more
women than men in church?

Because women are wiser than men.

Also because women have more free time than men do. All they have to do is to be their children's nurses, doctors, lawyers, pastors, psychologists, scientists, artists, authors, and a mere million other things, twenty-four hours a day, while men are busy doing one really, really important thing, such as doing the math for an insurance company or designing a new meaningless word for a new car, for seven hours a day.

Because, although women are oversensitive, hysterical, and crazy, men are stupid, selfish, stubborn, arrogant jerks.

Seriously, women are more intuitive and receptive to the supernatural than men are. Prepubescent children are also more receptive to the supernatural than teenagers are. For instance, women and children much more frequently encounter angels than men do.

Women are different from men (1) biologically, in obvious ways, (2) psychologically, because the body and the psyche always leave strong ripples in each other, and (3) mentally, because their brains are different in at least fifty-one ways.

I dare to utter this heretical truth because I am not the president of Harvard University and will not be fired for saying that we perhaps ought to at least discuss the possibility that women freely choose, rather than are compelled, to enter the hard sciences less often than men because women are by nature different in some way from men in mind as well as in body. (Google "Larry Summers" for the unbelievable story.)

The obvious biological difference is that a woman receives a man into her body, not vice versa. To anyone whose mind goes beyond mathematics, there is an obvious analogy between receiving God and receiving a man. God is (metaphorically, and rightly, though not literally) "He" not because the image of God is not male *and female* but because to God all souls are feminine.

Women's psychology is geared to and good at relationships, at welcoming, and at communities — at enclosing, like a womb. These are essential dimensions of religion. Men's psychology is geared toward hunting, fighting, and creating — at penetrating, like a sword. These are natural dimensions of individualism and nonconformity. These are not culturally variable and created stereotypes but universal and natural cross-cultural archetypes. Our culture is the only one in history that denies them. But even in denying them, we admit them, in calling their demolition "transgressive."

Women's brains are more geared to mystical and religious experience than men's. They are more holistic and intuitive, rather than calculating and analytic.

Atheists argue against God more often than theists argue for Him. All religions entail faith.

Faith goes beyond reason and calculation. Faith that goes beyond reason and proof is deadly to hunting and fighting (and the scientific method) but essential to family stability, trust, and love.

Why are there more old people than young people in church?

Because young people are stupid, selfish, stubborn, arrogant know-it-alls. How do I know this? I was young once.

And because there is no "church hormone."

And because God is not a chum but a Father. You can run away from Him more easily than you can run away from your father on earth.

And because old people are trying to get into Heaven.

What can we do for the cause of reunion of all the churches?

Thomas Merton gives us the answer. He writes: "We are not at peace with each other because we are not at peace with ourselves, and we are not at peace with ourselves because we are not at peace with God." That applies to relations between individuals, between nations, and between denominations.

It was sin and selfishness that divided us, so it will be holiness and love that reunites us. We split because we stopped following our common Conductor's baton. We know that His will is unity, so our disunity must have come from substituting "my will be done" for "Thy will be done." And unity can come only from the opposite source.

So, Merton got it right: the first step is peace with God; total unity of our will to His; personal sanctity. Saints don't burn each other as heretics. Put a Mother Teresa in every denomination, and denominationalism will eventually end.

It has to.

Read 1 Corinthians 1.

St. Paul had zero tolerance for denominationalism. Unless he's not an apostle and a prophet, that's true of God too. How could a loving Father tolerate having His children alienated from one another? The demand for unity, for reconciliation, is as essential a part of the Gospel as is correct theology or social justice. In fact, it's a part of correct theology and a part of social justice.

I think Muslims are our number-one enemies. What do you think?

I try to think with "the mind of Christ," as St. Paul tells us to do (see 1 Cor. 2:16). And how do we know the mind of Christ? Through the Church that He established and gave the authority to teach in His name: "He who hears you hears me," He said to His apostles (Luke 10:16), who ordained successors, who are the bishops of the one, holy, catholic (universal), and apostolic Church.

And the Church does not agree with you.

The *Catechism of the Catholic Church*, the first official universal catechism since the Catechism of the Council of Trent compiled five hundred years ago, says that Muslims worship the same God we and the Jews do. The Koran lists ninety-nine names for God ("Allah" is simply the Arabic word for "the one God"), and all ninety-nine are in the Bible too. Muslims don't accept Christ as God, just as Jews don't, but they revere Him as a prophet, as sinless, as virgin born, as one who performed miracles, including raising the dead, and they believe He will judge the whole world at the end of time. That's all in the Koran. Muslims' relationship to God is much more fearful and distant than ours, and they are suspicious of the love and intimacy we have with God, but as far as it goes, much of their theology is true, because they learned who God was from the same people we did—namely, the Chosen People, the Jews.

Their morality is also similar in many respects, though not as focused on love. Their list of virtues and vices, do's and don'ts, is much the same as ours. And they practice their morality at least as seriously as we do. Most Muslims you meet in America are quite moral, honest, reliable people.

Of course, their historical track record of violence and war, beginning with Muhammad himself, is even worse than ours. But most Muslims today do not support violence and terrorism. The Koran says, "Allah hates the aggressor." You can find many warlike, primitive verses in the Koran—and also in the Old Testament.

Even if some Muslims see us as their enemy, we don't see them as ours. The enemy within is far more dangerous and destructive to us than the enemy without. Terrorists are horribly wicked, hate-filled people. But they can kill only our bodies; traitors and heretics can kill our souls. So can priests who molest children. If terrorists deserve electric chairs, bad priests deserve millstones.

You would be hard-pressed to find a single Muslim in the world who's pro-abortion. Or antifamily. Or pro–sexual revolution. You'll find wicked Muslims, just as you will find wicked Christians. But Christians — at least Catholics — have almost the same rate of murder, rape, abortion, divorce, adultery, fornication, sodomy, transgenderism, and just about every other possible perversion, as unbelievers do throughout most of Western civilization. We are no longer a distinctive people, as we were in the days of the early Church. Muslims, Evangelicals, Pentecostals, and Orthodox Jews are more distinctive in their lifestyles than we are. That's the main reason we're losing six times more people than we're gaining every year, while those countercultural groups are all gaining.

Pope St. John Paul II fought and won a greater battle working with the Muslims than the Christians won against them in the Battle of Lepanto half a millennium earlier. He did this at the United Nations Cairo conference in the 1990s by allying the Church with the Muslims in blocking a United States–sponsored regulation that would have required every nation to legalize abortion in order to receive any UN benefits or aid. The regulation would have passed otherwise. George Weigel, the pope's official biographer, said that the Catholic Church could win the culture war and get her social morality legalized by simply replacing every "Catholic" politician in Washington with a Muslim or a Mormon.

Are we losing our religious freedom?

No.

We can't.

It's inherent.

It depends on free will, which is inalienable. Neither laws nor prisons nor tortures can take that freedom away.

But we are losing our political freedom to do and spend and speak and even think as we will.

The former mayor of Boston refused to allow Chick-fil-A into Boston because its president did not believe in same-sex "marriage." The CEO of Google was fired for the same reason. Couples in England are not allowed to adopt or even to have foster children if they believe the Bible's condemnation of sodomy.

But political freedom is not the most important thing, for four reasons. First, you can have too much of it. Second, like power, it corrupts. (Why doesn't anybody remind us of that?) Think of spoiled brats, famous rock stars, and dictators. Third, it's what adolescents want, not mature adults. Fourth, it's not what lovers want. Lovers choose marriage over freedom. When you want to be free, you are no longer in love. Love binds itself. Love makes vows.

Interior freedom, spiritual freedom, requires curbs on external freedom, bodily freedom.

The opposite of freedom is addiction, and the most dangerous and powerful addiction is the addiction to our own feelings and desires coupled with the freedom to get whatever we desire with no consequences. In other words, the opposite of true freedom is false freedom, slavery, and addiction to our selfish passions, which the Devil's propaganda makes appear to us as freedom.

By the way, my definition of "propaganda" is "the *propa mate* for a *propa goose*."

Catholicism

Why are you a Catholic? Tell me how you got here. (Short version, please.)

The ultimate cause, of course, was God's grace and His love for a stupid, selfish sinner. (No, I'm not being humble or even modest, just realistic. You fit that description too.)

The proximate or immediate cause was my reading Church history, especially the premodern Christian writers, especially the early ones, the Church Fathers, to try to prove to myself that Jesus established a Protestant church that gradually went bad and heretical and pagan—that is, Catholic—in the Middle Ages until Luther and Calvin re-formed it and brought it back to the thing Jesus established. That essential Protestant claim is refuted by all of Church history, beginning in the New Testament. "He who hears you hears me" (Luke 10:16). "You are Peter, and on this rock I will build my church" (Matt. 16:18). "This is my body" (Matt. 26:26). "The Church is the pillar and ground of the truth" (see 1 Tim. 3:15). "A man is justified by works and *not* by faith alone" (James 2:24, emphasis added).

Here is a short list of distinctively Catholic beliefs that Protestants don't accept because they can't find them explicitly taught in the New Testament: justification by faith *and* good works; the authority of the visible Church; apostolic succession; popes;

Purgatory; the Marian doctrines; prayers to saints; the Mass; the "*ex opera operato*" power of the sacraments, especially Baptism; and above all Christ's Real Presence in the Eucharist. Not a single one of these was denied, or even controverted, argued against, or doubted by Christians for the first fifteen hundred years. There were no Protestants until Protestantism. There is perfect continuity in the development of Catholic theology. It has grown like leaves on a tree, from within, not like barnacles on a ship or like aliens that came from without.

I like to keep things simple. As I read Church history, I avoided trying to figure out the truth on every controversial issue that separates Protestants from Catholics (and from the Orthodox too, by the way, except for how far the primacy of the authority of the pope extends). Instead, I looked at the logically primary and central one, the premise for all the others as conclusions—namely, the authority of the tradition, or stuff handed down, by the visible institution that teaches all these things, the one, holy, universal, and apostolic Catholic Church.

Where did the Church come from? From Christ and His apostles or from heretics? Are they leaves or barnacles? If they are leaves, all tree huggers must hug them too. That's Catholicism. If they are barnacles, they have to be scraped off and destroyed. That's Protestantism.

It's a question of historical fact, not just theological argument. So you don't have to be a genius or a professional to find the true Church. You just have to know a little history.

Of the four marks of the Church—one, holy, catholic, and apostolic—holiness is perhaps the most impressive, especially among so many notorious sinners, past and present. If the Catholic Church is as heretical as Protestants have to believe, where did all those thousands of incredible saints come from? Read them.

Is that the mind of Christ or the mind of a heretic? Is that light or darkness, truth or falsehood?

I read John of the Cross as a teenager. I didn't understand what he wrote, but I knew it was holy, and good, and, above all, real, substantial, like a great mountain — not an idea, an ideology, an imagination, an opinion, a subjective thing in the mind. It's the nature of reality at its height.

What Mass do you go to?

Every Sunday, if I can, I go to either the old Latin Mass, which is heavy with beauty and holiness and reverence, or the Anglican Use Mass, which uses the approved Catholic version of the old Book of Common Prayer, which, next to the King James Bible, is the greatest masterpiece in the English language.

You say that God is all good, all wise, and all powerful. Does that mean that this must be really "the best of all possible worlds"? Doesn't that follow logically from Romans 8:28, which you love to quote: "All things work together for good for those that love God"?

No. But it's a very intelligent question, because that conclusion *almost* follows, but not quite. "Almost" because in that verse, "all things" includes bad things, both physically bad things—sufferings—and even morally bad things—sins. God lets both kinds of evil happen deliberately. He lets pains and tragedies happen even though He could stop them, and He lets us sin even though He could give us the grace to avoid sin. Why? For the same reason He does everything: for our own deep, true, best good.

We don't usually see either of those two divine strategies, the one about sufferings and the one about sins, but sometimes we do see glimpses. The obvious example is the greatest evil in history, the Crucifixion, which was both the greatest physical suffering, the greatest torture, ever devised, and also the greatest sin in history, the deliberate hate and murder of God Incarnate. Christians celebrate that event on a day they dare to call "*Good* Friday."

We see the great good—eternal salvation—that came from that great evil, and sometimes we see how lesser evils, both sufferings and sins, work out for our best good in the end (e.g., they both give us wisdom and humility). That even applies to sins. Sometimes we see how God lets us learn from our sins. Aquinas says that God is like a doctor who tolerates lesser diseases because he sees that the cure for them would lead to an even greater disease. The greater spiritual disease is usually pride. If God cleaned up all our other sins, we would be worse off, because pride is the worst sin and the most concealed. Proud people usually think they're humble; only humble people know they're proud.

Our experience contains both clues and counter-clues to Romans 8:28. It is obviously *hard* to believe, in light of appearances, but it is *possible* to believe it, as long as you admit that you don't see everything, especially in the long run—in other words, that you're not God. (What a shock that is!)

But it is more than possible to believe; it is also necessary to believe, for it logically follows from three divine attributes: God's unlimited goodness and goodwill, His unlimited power, and His unlimited wisdom; that is, from His omnibenevolence, omnipotence, and omniscience. Any God worth the name has those three divine attributes. Unlimited goodness wants what is best for us, unlimited power is able to get whatever He wants, and unlimited wisdom knows what that is and what the best way to it is.

But that does not make this the best of all possible worlds, because it would be a better world if we used our free will to choose only the good, and not evil.

This is not the best of all possible worlds for a second reason: because there is no such thing as the best of all possible worlds, just as there is no such thing as the highest finite number. You can always add one more number, and you can always add one more good thing to any finite world.

Here is a third reason why this is not the best of all possible worlds: Heaven is a much better world. A world where all things *are* good is better than a world where all things, including bad things, work together *for* good. The first world is Heaven, and the second world is earth.

If you were pope, what is the
first thing you would do?

Resign.
That's the only way the Church and I would both survive.

If you were a priest and your parish was dying, what would you do about it?

I have a very concrete answer to that. I would begin where God began when He created the universe: with His Word, who is the Second Person of the Trinity, who became incarnate as Jesus Christ. I would begin with Christ. I would begin with adoration of Christ where He is now, in the Eucharist. I would begin with Eucharistic adoration. Every parish that did that resolvedly and with a strong will, and did not give up or compromise, has experienced a resurrection.

The reason is very simple and obvious: prayer works because God is real, and God answers prayer. Give yourself to Christ, and He will give Himself to you. The whole reason for a parish, the whole reason for the Mass, the whole reason for the Church, the whole reason for mankind, the whole reason for creating the universe was so that man could love and adore and worship God and receive His joy. Whether it is an individual or a parish that does this, things happen. Prayer, especially adoration, which is the essence of prayer, is not just an exercise within ourselves; it is a communication with God, and it is a two-way communication. When you put yourself in that relationship, it is like putting yourself in a great river. You are swept downstream. You do not emerge unchanged. Nor does your parish.

Jesus' disciples asked him many questions, but the one that made Him the happiest was: "Teach us to pray" (Luke 11:1).

His priests must teach that too.

And we all have to learn before we teach.

You said that Eucharistic adoration is
the first thing you would do to renew a
parish. Why is the Eucharist so central?

Because life is a Eucharist.

Too bad it has such a technical- and "churchy"-sounding
name. It is love; it is life; it is the whole meaning of our lives. It
is not just one very good thing in life, or in the world; life and
the world are in *it*.

It's not just that there is an analogy, a likeness; it's not just
that our life is *like* the Eucharist or that the Eucharist is like our
life. Rather, our life *is* a Eucharist.

What does "Eucharist" mean? It means what its Inventor
designed it to mean. It means: "Open your mouth and I will fill
it" (see Ps. 81:10). This applies to the Eucharist, and it applies
equally, in exactly the same way, to life. All good things—food
and water and air and pleasure and parents and children and
friends and animals—come from God, through a long chain
of intermediaries, from the Big Bang and evolution and human
history down through one minute ago. For it is the same God
(there's only one!) who fills our whole nature, body and soul, with
the same thing, His gifts, whenever we open the mouth of our
bodies and spirits. That's what faith and hope and love all are:

the opening of the mouths of our spirits. God keeps saying that to us every day and every moment: "Open your mouth and I will fill it." And we keep ignoring Him, because He comes in many disguises. He does this—He hides—to test and strengthen our faith, and He does that because faith and trust is the root of love.

The Eucharist is not just an *analogy* between matter and spirit, body and soul, a mere symbol. That's the Protestant idea of the Eucharist. It assumes the false Cartesian dualism of body versus soul as two separate things that might resemble each other. Do the words and the meaning of a book "resemble" each other? It's not just that in the Eucharist we open the mouths of our bodies and in life we open the mouths of our souls and wills, but in both we open both, together, at once. If we separate those two things and do not open both mouths, the Eucharist does not "take"; it does not hold. To receive the sacrament with body only and not soul, without faith and hope and charity, is sacrilege, not sacredness; and to receive God's will with our minds and imaginations but not act on it with our bodies is just as lame. For instance, to say, "I accept your commandment to feed the poor, but I will not share my life or my time or my food or my money with them" is not obedience but disobedience. Read James 2:14–16, and Christ's parable of the two brothers (Matt. 21:28–32): the one who said yes yet did not do his father's will, and the other one who said no yet did his father's will.

The Eucharist is neither a piece of material magic nor a mere spiritual thing, a symbol. It's one thing, not two, just as you and your body are one thing, not two, and as Christ and His Body are one thing, not two.

Christ's Body is the Church. That's not an analogy or a symbol either. Whatever I do to His Body, His people, I do to Him. He said that, not me.

The Eucharist is Jesus Christ Himself, in toto, both divinity and humanity, and in His humanity both soul and body, and in His body, both flesh and blood. We adore it because it is not an "it"; it is a "He," a Person, a divine Person. It is our God and our Savior Himself, in person, coming to us in unimaginable love and unsurpassable intimacy. That's all.

What's the reason for all the fuss you Catholics make about Mary?

As a Protestant, I just can't fathom why there's such a gulf between us about Mary. You Catholics seem to idolize her. Almost all Protestants feel you do. Could you explain it? I don't mean your dogmas about Mary — the Immaculate Conception and the Assumption — I know the arguments you have for them. But I sense there's something bigger, deeper, and more hidden in the soul about this whole Catholic schtick about Mary, whether it's right or wrong. Why is she a million times more important to you than she is to us? Can you explain it?

I understand your question, and it's a good one, because it perceives that our differences are not only about doctrine, about the dogmas. It's a sensibility, an intuition, a "big picture." Let me try to explain our side of the "big picture"; then you can explain yours and respond to ours if you like.

Every Catholic convert from Protestantism that I know of asks your question. Here's a very mysterious puzzle. On the one hand, the Marian doctrines are almost always the single hardest thing for a Protestant to understand and accept in Catholicism, the last obstacle.

But on the other hand, once converts have been Catholic for a long time, they look back on their Protestant objections and just can't understand why Mary was such an obstacle; she is so beautiful! What God did in her is so beautiful. She used to be the biggest minus to them, when they were Protestants, and now she's one of the biggest pluses. It's a change in sensibilities, and intuitions, and appreciations—not just the minds but the hearts.

They wonder, as I do, why Protestants don't see the beauty of it all and love Mary as much as Catholics do. They forget their Protestant sensibilities so completely that they just don't understand them anymore. That's true of me, and of almost all Protestant-to-Catholic converts I know. Check it out; ask them; nine out of ten will say the same thing.

So, I can't explain your side of the great divide, because I've forgotten how it used to look to me as a Protestant and why Mary was so unimportant to my Protestant sensibilities. All I can tell you is why she is now so important to me, to my Catholic sensibilities. The answer is a single word. Do you want to guess what the word is?

OK. For me, the word would be "idolatry," but I guess that's not the word for you. So, it must be "Church authority" or "tradition," right?

Nope. Try again.

The theology of grace using nature, perfecting nature?

Good guess, and that's involved in it too, I think, but no, that's not it. It's just one word.

I give up. What is it?

Jesus.

That's my favorite word too.

Good! If there's one thing Protestants really get, it's Chris-tocentrism, the all-importance of Jesus, loving Jesus, adoring Jesus, seeing Him as absolute Lord and Savior, as everything. There's another group of Christians who are like that too: all the Catholic saints. Not all the Catholics, but certainly all the Catholic saints. Unfortunately, not all Catholics are saints or even close to being saints.

Let me try to explain Mary by Jesus. Just as Mary never pointed to herself but only to Him, so all the doctrines about Mary are ways of praising not just Mary but Him. We love Mary for one reason: because we love Jesus. The more we love Jesus, the more we love Mary. If we could grade Catholics on a scale of sainthood, a kind of spiritual graph, three lines would be almost identical in height or depth: how saintly you are, how much you love Jesus, and how much you love Mary.

That's the empirical fact. Here comes the explanation.

Look at the Hail Mary prayer. It stops halfway through. The speaker has to take a silence break before and after the name "Jesus." He's at the heart of that prayer as He was at the heart of her body, her womb. Look at the title we give her in that prayer: "Mother of God." Unbelievable, astonishing, incredible, amaz-ing, infinitely wonderful! What? Jesus in Mary, Jesus incarnating, Jesus coming down to us *in Mary.*

Suppose He had chosen to come in another way. He could have. He could have appeared instantly as a full-grown man descending from the sky, the reverse of the Ascension. He could have come down on a mountaintop, or in the Temple. And if he had, every Christian in the world who adored Him would make a pilgrimage to that mountain or that Temple. They would love that place above all places in the universe. They would make a very big deal of it. Why? *Because they make a very big deal about Him.*

Well, why not do the same with Mary? She is the place where the single most important and miraculous and wonderful thing that ever happened, happened. It's what C. S. Lewis called "the grand miracle." It's far greater than the creation of the universe. The eternal, immortal, infinite God became a temporal, mortal, finite man out of love of us, for our salvation. Wow! The sparks from that "Wow" are what fires up our love of Mary.

Here's the same point from another prayer, the Angelus. The second stanza starts with these two sentences word for word from the Gospels: "Behold the handmaid of the Lord; be it done unto me according to thy word" (see Luke 1:38). And the next sentence says, "And the Word became flesh, and dwelt among us." Look how it juxtaposes those two sentences. The second sentence is the most amazing sentence ever uttered. It tells us the most amazing thing that ever happened: God became man. And the sentence before that tells us why, tells us the cause: it was this woman's free Yes to God's invitation. It was God's invitation, of course; the angel was only the mailman. And it was not a command, it was an invitation, and she could have refused it, and if she had, then no one could ever have gone to Heaven. Her words were "Be it done to me according to Your Word." "Fiat." "Let it be." The same word God spoke to create the entire universe. The word of power. The word that released the Word, the Word of God, the Second Person of the Eternal Trinity, Jesus Christ, the Lord of the world, our Savior and our only hope, our everything. The greatest thing that ever happened, happened *in her* and *because of her*.

So, you see, the more we love and adore Jesus, the more we love and reverence Mary. We just can't stop it. We love Him infinitely; we love Him far too much not to love her as much as any creature can be loved because she is as good and as beautiful as any creature can be.

What's the reason for all the fuss you make about Mary?

That's where we're coming from. And all the Eastern Orthodox churches too. Even Muslims love her and revere her more than Protestants do, for her perfect "islam," her perfect surrender to God. I hope you Protestants can use your Christian imagination and your Christian empathy to understand that crazy, wild love of ours. Yes, our love for Mary is crazy and wild, because God's love for us is crazy and wild. And God's love for us happened *in her*, first in making her immaculate when He created her soul at her conception, to prepare her for her perfect Yes, and then in making her the Mother of God in the Incarnation — which, by the way, happened not on Christmas, December 25, but on March 25, nine months before Christmas. We make a big deal out of Christmas; we should make an even bigger deal out of March 25. The greatest event in history, the Incarnation, happened at the Annunciation, not the Nativity.

How can Protestants and Catholics understand one another better when we think of Mary?

Oh, I think there are a lot of things we can both do, and most of them are pretty obvious and commonsensical, starting with listening openly and honestly to each other. That's number 1. And praying to God to enlighten our minds. That's number 2. And opening our hearts to His will, whatever and wherever it is. That's number 3, and that's the secret of discernment, you know. Jesus solved the problem of how to discern God's will and God's mind in John 7:17 in a way that was terribly easy to understand and terribly difficult to practice. He said to the Jews who asked Him how they could understand His teaching and how they could know it was from God, "If your will were to do the will of my Father, you would understand my teaching, and that it is from Him."

Those are just three starting principles, and there are many more, but they're true of every issue that divides us. Mary is different, because the most powerful and the most effective answer to the question about Mary is not something we ought to do in the future but something she is doing right now in the present. She is praying passionately to her Son that we be one, that His passionate high-priestly prayer in John 17 be answered, quickly and powerfully and definitively. She will unite the Church by her love and her prayers, because they are real, and they are much more powerful and perfect than our love and our prayers. The Devil fears her more than he fears the rest of the Church as a whole. She whupped him in Jerusalem, and she whupped him again at Lepanto, and she whupped him again in Mexico as Our Lady of Guadalupe, and there is nowhere he can hide, and he is terrified of this little woman.

You think Mary divides us? Mary will unite us! She will unite us by the power of her prayers and tears. She weeps when she sees her children divided and her Son's visible body torn into thirty thousand denominations. And those tears are a spiritual tidal wave.

(Significantly, the large audience who heard the above answer, which was composed of almost as many Protestants as Catholics, was friendly and smiling and comfortable during all the previous discussion of this divisive issue, but everyone suddenly became very quiet and serious looking when I said what I said in the last two paragraphs. Our hearts are wiser than our heads.)

Why does the Church resist women's ordination?
That seems to most people, even most educated
Catholics, to be a prime example of being on
the wrong side of history, because it insults
women. It denies equality. It's male chauvinism,
keeping women out of the old-boy network.

Judaism is the only ancient religion that has no priestesses and
no goddesses. Its one God is not one of many and not one part
of the cosmos but the transcendent Creator. He is other than
the cosmos, as a man is other than a woman. The universe does
not come out of Him like a baby out of a woman or a web out of
a spider. He comes into the universe from this position of other-
ness, from without, by creating it, knowing it, loving it, sending
prophets into it, and performing miracles in it. This is why all
Jewish and Christian and Muslim literature uses masculine pronouns for God. Obviously, God is not literally, biologically male
because God does not have a body; God is not a biological being.

Priests have two essential tasks: they mediate between God
and mankind, representing mankind to God and God to mankind.
There is no reason a priest cannot be female as far as representing
mankind to God, because women and men are equal, equally
good, equally holy, and equally the image of God according to

Genesis 1:27. But if God is a "He," then the other function of a priest requires that a priest be a "he." It is simply misleading for a man to play a queen or a woman to play a king.

Christians do not correct Christ. Christ ordained no women among His apostles, even though He had many woman followers, and they remained more faithful to Him than His men did when He was crucified: all ran away except John. Jesus treated women with far greater respect than His culture did.

So, it makes no sense to say what feminists who want to be priestesses say: that Jesus was a victim of His cultural biases. He did not hesitate to shock and contradict His culture on any other issue; why would He succumb to male chauvinism if He is the infallible God and not a fallible, fallen man?

When St. John Paul II ended the debate on priestesses by saying that the Church does not have the authority to do so, he invoked the formula of apostolic authority, which makes that an infallible and irreformable teaching. If you are a Catholic, you let your Church correct you; you do not correct your Church. As Chesterton said, we do not need a church to tell us we are right when we are right; we need a church to tell us we are wrong when we are wrong.

Marriage and Sexuality

What is marriage and why is it so great?

Marriage is the craziest and most wonderful thing you can do.

It's the world's most challenging and complicated institution, for two reasons.

The first is that only in marriage do you give your whole self to another person, body and soul, forever.

The second reason is that you do that in religion too, but in religion one of the two persons (God) is *not* stupid, selfish, shallow, and stubborn.

God is perfect. You ain't. (Quick! Call the reporters!) And neither is the person you are at first so in love with that you see him or her as a god or goddess. That's your foretaste, your forepeek, at Heaven, not earth.

Since there is in this world no such thing as a perfect human being, there is no such thing as a perfect marriage. (Yet we long for such perfection, which means that our hearts are programmed for it, eventually.) We are all damaged goods. (If, when getting married, you didn't know that you were getting a car with flat tires for the only ride in your life that never really ends short of death, you'd be a fool.)

Of course, there's always suicide.

Divorce is suicide: of the new "one-flesh," "two-in-one" person you co-created by marriage.

It's also deadly for your victims, the new little persons you procreate. Nothing predicts future failure in life for your kids better than your suicide by divorce.

Falling in love is wonderful, but it makes you a fool.

But if you never do it, you are an even bigger fool.

Fools can choose to marry other fools (there are no other candidates); and they can stay alive, stay married for life; and that is even more wonderful, more amazing, than falling in love in the first place.

Marriage is designed for fools. We need each other. We are drunks who would fall down if we didn't hold each other up.

Marriage also produces kids, if you let it.

When God says, "The two shall become one flesh," that's the one He means, the one that the two become: the child.

That's why you were brought into existence, and that's why you bring others into existence: you "pay it forward." You can't give your parents a gift equal to the gift they gave you: you can't give them life. So, you pass it on.

Life is a relay race. That's what God designed sex *for*: nothing less than the most Godlike thing you can do. You can't create, but you can procreate. And that's why He made it so pleasant and so intimate. And that's what makes it so crazy and wonderful.

Why not trial marriages — living together? Everybody does it today, even Catholics. It should cut down on divorce. Isn't it better for marriage if you discover your incompatibilities before rather than after getting married? Buying a car without test driving it is irresponsible.

And with what result? They are five times more likely to divorce.

Why aren't women insulted by being compared to cars? Why do women let themselves be used and abused by men in the hookup culture? It makes every college a selfish sex addict's dream: it turns an educational institution into a free whorehouse.

We don't know what marriage is anymore, just as we don't know what sex is anymore. So, we talk about "same-sex marriage," which is like talking about "jumbo shrimp" or "military intelligence" or "the philosophy of skepticism." ("Philosophy" means "the love of wisdom," not the denial of it.) We don't even know the single most basic truth about sex, because we call babies "accidents." So, the primary effect of our "sex education" is ignorance of the single most important fact about sex. Soon we will relabel all the anatomy books, and what used to be called "the reproductive system" will be called "the sexual stimulation system."

Nearly every couple who marries nowadays does so with one goal in mind: personal happiness. That's like enlisting in the army for personal happiness, or building a bridge for personal happiness. Marriage is a vocation, an enterprise, a work. It has products, which is its point and its center. They are called children. That's how you came into the world—unless you came out of a test tube.

If you don't want to give your whole life to your spouse and to your children, if you don't want your whole life to be changed and be no longer your own, don't marry. And don't convert to any religion either, because every religion also tells you that you are not your own; you are totally relative to something like God. And don't even try to be moral, because the essence of morality is unselfishness, charity, the gift of self to others, self-forgetful love of others. Morality, religion, marriage, and family all go together. And they are all going down the drain together today. They all put curbs on your freedom and autonomy, on your desire to be God. And the God you want to be is not the God who is self-giving love but the god who is a spoiled, selfish, immature brat.

If you don't want to fit that profile, convert, marry, and give yourself away. You will be one of the few deeply happy people left in the Brave New World.

Why does the Catholic Church forbid divorce?

Answer 1: The Church doesn't forbid it; she denies that it exists. "What God has joined together, let not man put asunder" (Mark 10:9). No man *can* do that; he can only pretend to. Divorce, like ghouls, vampires, and werewolves, is a superstition. It does not exist. It is a lie. A valid marriage is for life. An invalid marriage cannot be dissolved by divorce because it is not a marriage to begin with and can only be annulled, i.e., declared to be invalid from the beginning.

Answer 2: Unlike all other churches, the Catholic Church does not have enough arrogance to believe she has the authority to contradict her master, Christ, who clearly taught "no divorce" in all three synoptic Gospels.

Divorce, Italian Style is the title of a very funny sixties movie. Back then, divorce simply did not exist in Italy, since Italy was a Catholic country. So, if an Italian man of the sixties wanted to divorce his wife, he had to do it Italian style, which was murder. He had to find a hit man. In the movie, the protagonist, who wants to get rid of his wife, does just that. But the wife is just about the only woman who does *not* get whacked by this supremely clumsy hit man.

My wife and I found this movie not only hilarious but cheery, because we both thought that murder was much more reasonable than divorce; so as long as we didn't have any lethal instruments in the house, we would be safe forever. That door labeled "divorce" was never open. That has given us (and our kids) a great sense of security.

Answer 3: The Church hates divorce for the same reason Christ does: she loves children, who are more hurt by the divorce of their parents than by their parents' death. Kids are often morally wiser than adults are. They think people should keep their solemn promises.

How silly kids are!

Why won't the Church allow divorced and remarried Catholics to receive the Eucharist? Do you think Pope Francis will change that?

You're right to put those two questions together, and in the right order. The answer to the one gives you the answer to the second. But I want to back up for a minute to the first question. In order to answer it, you have to understand that two of the most important things in the whole world are the Catholic Faith, and marriage, sex, and the family, because they both come from God and because they are the two most common and universal things bigger than we are that make us holy. They are the two things the Devil hates the most on this earth.

The Church's teaching has two parts: principles and practice. Her principles come from God, not from man. They are dogmas—that is, divinely given data. That's why they are unchangeable. The Church's practice can and does change, because those unchangeable principles need to be applied in changing ways to changing situations. Who is allowed to receive the Eucharist is a matter of practice, and it has, in fact, changed somewhat in history. For instance, at what age can one receive First Communion? And how long a fast is required for it? And can those who were forbidden to receive Communion during their lives ever receive

Communion at the point of death if they want it and believe in it? (The answer to that question is yes, by the way.)

On the other hand, the Church's dogmas limit her practice. She might someday allow intercommunion with Eastern Orthodox Christians, who have valid sacraments and who believe in the Real Presence, but not with Protestants, who do not. The latter would be like allowing someone to play with a holy thing, or to treat it as less holy than it is. Like sex. The Church would probably make millions of converts if she said that it is OK to play with sex as mere entertainment, but she can't do that, out of love and loyalty to this beautiful thing God invented as the way of procreating eternal, infinitely valuable things called persons.

Until we know what her dogmatic principles are concerning marriage and divorce and reception of the Eucharist, we can't know whether her practice can change about divorced and remarried Catholics receiving Communion.

There are three main principles involved here. The first is that marriage is a divine institution and a sacrament. It is a sign and symbol of our marriage to Christ, which is the whole meaning of life, and our ultimate hope and destiny.

The second principle follows from that: that a valid sacramental marriage is indissoluble, because Christ's marriage covenant with His Church, His Mystical Body, is indissoluble. Christ will never, never abandon His Bride. There can be no divorce on earth because marriage is an image of Heaven and there is no divorce in Heaven.

Christ Himself clearly forbade divorce, in three of the four Gospels. When Protestants ask me why the Catholic Church is so arrogant that she refuses to acknowledge divorce, I reply that she is not as arrogant as all the other churches that do, thereby directly disobeying a direct command of the person they claim to be their Lord. We only deliver Christ's mail; we do not edit it.

The third principle is that marriage demands fidelity, so that adultery is clearly a mortal sin.

These three principles stand or fall together. If the third is denied, this denies the second, and if the second is denied, this denies the first.

One more principle: "mortal sin" means two things: (1) an act that by its own nature is so serious that it can kill the eternal life in your soul, and (2) the state of a soul that lacks that life. You can't go to Hell for a little act of unkindness to your spouse, but you can go to Hell for being an adulterer, if you do it knowingly and willingly rather than ignorantly and unwillingly, and do not repent.

Let's now add a principle about practice: no one in a state of mortal sin should be given the Eucharist. Now, no one except God knows for certain whether any given soul is personally and subjectively in a state of mortal sin and deprived of divine life. If a person died in that state at this moment, he could not go to Heaven—not because God keeps him out but because he keeps himself out. He would not be able to endure Heaven or to enjoy it. Now, not everyone who has committed adultery is in a state of mortal sin, but it is very clear that, objectively speaking, adultery is a mortal sin. So one cannot receive the Eucharist if one is living in adultery and does not repent and leave that adulterous relationship (because repenting is not just a feeling but an act, or at least a firm and honest resolution to act or not to act).

What Pope Francis is saying is, first, that it ought to be simpler and less expensive for Catholics whose first marriage was not valid to get an annulment, a declaration of nullity, which allows them to enter a second marriage, a valid one. The process was complicated, long, and expensive, and that discouraged people, especially the poor. It was like waiting in a very long line to get X-rayed. But without the X-ray, without the truth about whether the first marriage was valid, you couldn't proceed and make informed choices.

And second, Francis is emphasizing that the Church should not give up on Catholics who are civilly divorced from their first marriages and have not yet gotten annulments and who have married again or who are living with and having sex with persons they are not validly married to in the eyes of the Church. He is saying that the Church should "accompany" them pastorally and psychologically, and be understanding and compassionate toward them, without denying any of the Church's principles, and that they should be encouraged to participate in the Church in all the ways that the Church allows them to, up to but not including the reception of the Eucharist. That's what Jesus Christ would do. That's the ultimate reason for everything the Church does. The two things the Church absolutely insists on are truth and love, because those are the two things Christ insists on and because those are two of the things God is in His essential nature. That's why we should all love sinners much more than we do and should hate sins much more than we do—for that very same reason we love sinners: because sins harm them. So it's precisely out of love for them that we must tell them the truth. We can never give up on them any more than Jesus did. He even called Judas Iscariot "friend" when he betrayed Him in the garden. When a friend has a problem, we try to fix it for him. The Church is in the people fix-it business. But we can't fix anything without truth, just as we can't do surgery without light.

Pope Francis is big on mercy and compassion and pastoral care—like Jesus, and like all the saints. Unfortunately, he's not an intellectual, and he's not very clear about dogma. But he can't change dogma. Even the wicked Renaissance popes couldn't do that. The Holy Spirit does not allow it.

Bottom line: Can the Church allow any Catholics who are civilly divorced and remarried, without their first marriage having been annulled by the Church, to receive the Eucharist? Since this is a matter of pastoral practice, I'm not sure, though I strongly believe the answer has to be no, because I don't see how that practice can change without violating one of the principles on which it is based, and I am quite sure that the Church cannot and will not change any of those principles.

How can I tell if I love someone?

If you don't know what love is, you can't tell. If you don't know what a gold nugget is, you won't be able to tell whether you've found one or whether it's only fool's gold.

Love is to will the good of another person. Love is not a feeling. Feelings help cause it, but it is essentially a free choice. Feelings help get it started, but it stays and grows only by a continual choice of the will. Feelings also result from it—loving always makes you deeply happy—but love only for the sake of your own private feelings is not to love the other but to love yourself.

Since we live in a material world, and two material things can't occupy the same space at the same time, one state of affairs in the physical world is a benefit to one and a loss to another. For instance, my shield stops your sword; the more taxes I pay, the richer the government is; and if I give you half my pizza, I have only half a pizza left. Love always means the willingness to sacrifice your stuff and space and time for another person. The surest test of love is sacrifice. That's true of all kinds of love: erotic love, friendship, philanthropy, altruism, liking, goodwill, admiration, compassion—all kinds of love are proved by actions, not by feelings.

But by a wonderful paradox, the more love you give, the more you have left over. And the more you work for someone else's happiness, forgetting your own, the happier you are. That's not just an ideal or a principle; that's a fact of experience.

If you are trying to decide whether you love someone enough to marry that person, ask yourself this question: Do I really want to give my whole self and my whole life to that person? If so, marry him or her; if not, don't. If you think you will be absolutely miserable with that person, don't marry; but don't marry for your own happiness, because that always backfires. That other person is not a means to your happiness but an end in himself or herself. Two people who marry out of the firm desire to give their whole selves to each other and not out of the desire for personal happiness — that is, people who look at the other person as an end, not as a means to happiness — will be happy. It's often said that happiness is a bird: if you chase it, it flies away, and if you grab it, you kill it.

And if each of the two wants to live and give and sacrifice for the other one, both should be just as willing to live and give and sacrifice for their children. That's the double meaning of marriage. It's a call, a vocation, a high and holy job — like joining the army or becoming a priest. You exist for the job; the job does not exist for you. It's a big deal; it's like an elephant. It's like the universe: it's not our invention, and you can't change it into what it's not. You conform to it; it does not conform to you.

You don't have to ride on the elephant, but if you do, you can't turn it into a donkey.

We're both sexually addicted and sexually confused. What is sex?

Sex has been changed from something we are to something we do, or something we "get." What used to be our natural identity has been reduced to our chosen activity. And that activity has been so cut off from its nature and natural end that babies are reduced to either "choices" or "accidents."

What we used to call sex we now call merely gender. "Gender" used to be a term in grammar. It meant that there were not two kinds of people but two kinds of nouns.

So, our sexual identity has been eviscerated and cut in two, reduced to grammar plus orgasm.

We are nouns that copulate.

Before the "sexual revolution," everyone knew that sex is a pervasive, natural, and important dimension of what we are. We are masculine or feminine. Those words always meant something real, clear, different, strong, and good. Now it is a heresy to say they mean anything at all, especially that men and women are different "by nature"—even though there are at least fifty-one biological differences between the masculine human brain and the feminine human brain; even though all of our funniest sexual jokes make no sense at all if the modern view is correct.

You hear all the time that it is an old superstition that men are by nature superior to women. If that was only a superstition, major league baseball teams would include women.

You hear all the time that it is an old superstition that women are by nature superior to men. If that was only a superstition, men would have babies. They would also know how to make them stop crying. But men don't even know how to make women stop crying.

If there was nobody superior to you, how could you ever have any admiration or respect or humility toward anybody? Sex teaches us life's most important lesson: that we are not God, that we need each other, and therefore most respect and admire and even love each other. It's a "Duh!" Or rather, it used to be.

Why is the Catholic Church obsessed with sex?

She's not.

Her critics are.

Imagine a drug-addicted teenager whose parents gently remind him once a month that he is ruining his life with drugs. The teenager says to his mother (Holy Mother Church is our mother) what you are saying to the Church: Why are you so obsessed with drugs?

It's what psychologists call projection. It's like yodeling in a canyon: the voice you hear is an echo of your own.

So that's my first answer to your question. The Church isn't obsessed with sex; the secular culture is.

Second, the Church is profoundly right to be "obsessed" with this obsession because the sexual revolution is ruining Western culture, ruining families, ruining souls, and ruining personal happiness, peace, and joy.

The Church is obsessed with one thing. The Church is obsessed with God, and with union with God.

Sexual union is a little, pale, distant, tiny icon, or holy picture, of *that*.

God is the only obsession that does not enslave us; it frees us, because God is love, and love always frees the beloved.

Addicts don't appreciate their addiction. Alcoholics have destroyed their enjoyment of alcohol. The Bible says that God invented wine "to gladden the heart of man" (Ps. 104:15). Addiction turns gladdening into saddening. We've done the same with sex. We're not enjoying it anymore. It's not really sexy. That's why we have to up the ante: the addict has to double the dose constantly to get the same buzz.

And it always fails.

St. Thomas Aquinas says that sexual pleasure in Eden, in innocence, was far more intense, far more pleasurable, than it is now. The closer we get to that state of unselfish, natural, spontaneous, innocent, sinless, totally self-giving and self-forgetful love that is the essence of being a saint and the essence of our future joy in Heaven—the closer we get to that now, the more joy we have.

The greatest "joy of sex" is not orgasm. Even animals experience that. It's personal intimacy. (I speak from the perspective of a man, so I'll use sexist pronouns, since I'm talking about sex.) It's the realization that this beautiful person whom you love like crazy also loves you like crazy and invites you into the deepest recesses, the most interior secret, the walled garden, of herself, both body and soul at once, the totality of herself, including her fertility and the whole rest of her life, including her children, which will be your children too. That's the "one flesh" the two become: children, new human beings, more infinitely valuable eternal souls. What could possibly be more wonderful and exciting and sexy than that? The sexual revolution has depersonalized sex, changed it from a "thou" into an "it." Sex used to mean something we are; now it means only something we do.

Just as so-called feminism has robbed us of femininity, the sexual revolution has robbed us of sex.

I'm told that the second most successful book in the world, after the Bible, is *The Joy of Sex*. But the Bible and the Church (which go together like the textbook and the teacher) wrote the real, true, original version of *The Joy of Sex*. The Devil always substitutes joyless imitations for joyful originals. That's because he's not creative; only God is. God produces the version; he produces the perversion. Perversions always lessen the joy. The inventor of all obsessions is not the Church; it's the Devil.

I saw a book in a bookstore once entitled *The Catholic Sex Book*. It was a blank book. That's supposed to be a joke, but it's a joke on the jokester. It's the Devil's sex book that's blank. The Catholic sex book is thick and full of color. One version of it is St. John Paul ll's Theology of the Body. I challenge anyone who thinks the Church is anti-sex to explore that. I guarantee that your mind will be blown and expanded and changed.

Another part of the answer is that the Church seems, to our secular culture, to be obsessed with sex because she is obsessed with holiness, and sex is holy. Sex is holy because sex is part of the image of God, according to the Bible (read Genesis 1:27). Sex is holy because it is the way God designed to perform the greatest miracle in this world: the creation of the only thing in the universe that is intrinsically valuable, that is to be loved for its own sake, as an end and not as a means, that has infinite value and that is destined to possess eternal life, supernatural life, to participate in the very life of the Trinity.

That's what sex is about, what it really is. What sex *feels like* to you and what sex is *desired for* by us today—namely. the most intense pleasure most of us ever experience in life—is not identical with what sex *is*. God attached the power and the pleasure together—the power to procreate and the pleasure of creating.

He did this for a good reason: because objectively great things deserve subjectively great joys.

It's quite natural to be obsessed with sexual pleasure, to become a sex addict. That's always been so, in every culture and every religion or anti-religion in history. Human nature doesn't essentially change. But human philosophies and ideologies do. The "sexual revolution" didn't change sexual desire or even sexual behavior as much as it changed sexual thinking, sexual philosophy. It's no longer the reproductive system; it's the entertainment system. Children are accidents. That's exactly like saying that growth is an accident of eating, or that wisdom is an accident of learning, or arriving is an accident of traveling. It's like saying that seeing is an accident of opening your eyes.

What's the essence of the Theology of the Body?

Glad you put in that qualification about the essence of it. If you hadn't, I would have had to talk for the next week. John Paul II is a saint but not an easy writer. When you investigate this theology, start with Christopher West, who is not quite as profound and saintly but is a better writer.

The essence of the Theology of the Body is a "big picture" of sexuality as holy, as an icon, a holy picture of the love life of the Trinity, as an essential dimension of the image of God in us. Everything else follows from that, both positive and negative, both the goodness and joy and positivity of sexual identity and sexual activity and sexual pleasure and the need for strong rules about not adulterating it, including the defense of and the explanation for *Humanae Vitae*.

The best introduction to a deep subject is a short one.

Why are children important?

Answer 1: Because children are the fulfillment of life. Children are the fulfillment of life because they are the fulfillment of marriage, and marriage is the fulfillment of love, and love is the fulfillment of life.

Answer 2: Because we don't matter as much as we think we do, but children matter more than we think they do. In fact, if children don't matter, then none of us matter, because none of us came into the world except as children.

Answer 3: Because to God we are all children.

Why is the Catholic Church the only church that forbids birth control? If that's not an obsession with rules and prohibitions, I don't know what is.

Well, then, I guess you don't know what is. Let me try to tell you.

The Church is not opposed to birth control. Natural family planning is natural birth control, and everyone who practices it loves it, even though it's not easy and takes effort. Half of the people who use it are non-Catholics, by the way. And the divorce rate among people who practice it is between 1 and 2 percent as compared with a 50 percent divorce rate among everyone else. If you think that's an accident, you probably think that children are an accident of sex—oops, I forgot, that's exactly what you *do* think. Well, maybe you'd like to buy my time-share in Florida.

Let me try to explain it not by abstract arguments but by a concrete analogy. Imagine a priest who loves to say Mass but is afraid of Jesus Christ. He doesn't want Christ to come and transubstantiate the bread and wine into His own Body and Blood. He wants to lock the door to one of the two greatest miracles (and one of the two most frequent miracles) God performs in the world—namely, transubstantiation. (The other miracle is conception, procreation.) So, when it comes to the words of consecration, "This is my Body" and "This is my Blood," this priest moves his lips and pretends to say the words, but he doesn't say them. He fakes it. He lies, at the most solemn moment of his life and his work. Wouldn't that be blasphemous? Well, that's what artificial contraception does. It puts a lock on the door so God can't come in. It puts a condom on God, so He can't interfere and create a new human being. It responds to God's knock on the door by locking the door. It says: "You attached the pleasure to the miracle, and I separated them because I want the pleasure but not the miracle." Exactly like the lying, faking priest.

Contraception is not birth control; it's birth prevention. It's wrong not because it's artificial but because it's antinatural. And nature here does not mean just matter, or biology; it means the nature of sex, which is the total gift of man and woman to each other, soul and body, and part of the body is its fertility. "I give you my whole self, my heart and my life, and my body, and my children and my future with them and with you." That's what sex actually, really, objectively *is*. If we don't want that, we don't want what sex really is. We want something else. What sex says with its body is total self-giving, but what contraceptive sex says with its mind and will is the opposite: I withhold this miraculous power of myself. I give you only the appearance, not the reality. I lie with my body. I hold back my most miraculous and precious power. I'm prudent and rational and controlled and scientific and mechanical and pragmatic and utilitarian. I'm not wild and crazy and romantic and risky and dramatic. I don't want the lion; I want the kitten. I'm not a poet and a mystic, I'm a tame little pet.

What's the difference between NFP and contraception?

It's the same as the difference between a natural death and mercy killing. The right thing is not to play God but to let God decide in matters of life and death, at both ends of life, the beginning and the end.

What's wrong with masturbation? It makes no sense to me. It's natural and universal, and it causes only harmless pleasure and release from frustration, and it hurts nobody.

The answer is simple and obvious, once you see it. I quote a C. S. Lewis letter on this:

> For me the real evil of masturbation would be that it takes an appetite which, in lawful use, leads the individual out of himself to complete (and correct) his own personality in that of another (and finally in children and even grandchildren) and turns it back: sends the man back into the prison of himself, there to keep a harem of imaginary brides. And this harem, once admitted, works against his ever getting out and really uniting with a real woman. For the harem is always accessible, always subservient, calls for no sacrifices or adjustments, and can be endowed with erotic and psychological attractions which no real woman can rival. Among those shadowy brides he is always adored, always the perfect lover: no demand is made on his unselfishness, no mortification ever imposed on his vanity. In the end, they become merely the medium through which he increasingly adores himself....

And it is not only the faculty of love which is thus sterilized, forced back on itself, but also the faculty of imagination. The true exercise of imagination, in my view, is (a) to help us to understand other people, (b) to respond to, and for some of us, to produce, art. But it also has a bad use: to provide for us, in shadowy form, a substitute for virtues, successes, distinctions, etc., which ought to be sought *outside* in the real world, e.g., picturing all I'd do if I were rich instead of earning and saving.

Masturbation involves this abuse of imagination in erotic matters (which I think bad in itself) and thereby encourages a similar abuse of it in all spheres. After all, almost the main work of life is to come out of ourselves, out of the little, dark prison we are all born in. Masturbation is to be avoided as all things are to be avoided which retard this process. The danger is that of coming to love the prison.[3]

---

[3] Lewis to Keith Masson, March 6, 1956, in *The Collected Letters of C. S. Lewis*, vol. 3, *Narnia, Cambridge and Joy 1950–1963*, ed. Walter Hooper (San Francisco: HarperSanFrancisco, 2007), 758–759.

Why do people want to change their gender?

Because the Devil hates them and hates their happiness, so he confuses them by making them hate something good, something God designed and made, something natural: their bodies. The Devil hates everything natural, because God created it. So the Devil always loves to pervert natural things. Remember that scene toward the end of the movie *The Shining*, where Jack Nicholson sees the Devil's work in the spirits in that haunted hotel. Dogs have men's faces, and men have dogs' faces. The Devil loves that for the same reason he wants men to hate their masculinity and pretend to be women, and women to hate their femininity and pretend to be men. The Devil loves all lies. He is "the father of lies" (see John 8:44). He especially loves to corrupt innocence and childhood; therefore, he loves child abuse, especially by priests, who rape children's souls as well as bodies, instead of saving them, or by doctors who surgically mutilate a child's sex organs instead of psychologically healing their minds. We are increasingly living in that movie.

Our attitude toward transgender people should be the same as our attitude toward wounded soldiers. The Church is indeed a field hospital on a battlefield, as Pope Francis has famously said. She exists for the wounded. The only qualification for membership in the Church is to be wounded. We all qualify.

Ask Peter Kreeft

We should be compassionate toward people who want to change their gender. We cannot help them if we do not listen to them and understand them. They feel that their souls are in the wrong bodies, that God made a mistake, that they know who they really are more than He does. They need to find peace and unity in their identity. And the way to do that is not to attack their bodies, as if they were mistakes, as if their sex organs were enemies that had to be killed, but to treat their souls, their minds and feelings, by psychiatry. We could all benefit from psychiatry. You don't have to be crazy to need psychiatry. Or, alternatively, we're all crazy. And Jesus is the greatest psychiatrist.

Spiritual Life

How can we have joy when our lives are full of misery?

A visitor to the little French town of Chartres in the Middle Ages was walking through rain and mud one cold winter day when he saw hundreds of peasants struggling to pull enormous stones through the mud on rollers, inch by inch. Many of them were cursing.

"What are you doing?" he asked one.

"I'm trying to get these damn stones to move through this damn mud!" he replied, his face full of sweat.

The visitor noticed one peasant who was struggling just as much as the others but was not cursing. In fact, he was singing. "What are you doing?" asked the visitor.

The peasant answered, "I'm building a cathedral."

Here is a modern version of the above, borrowed from Andrea Black.

We often ask, when we are going to the hospital or paying the bills or visiting Grandma in a nursing home or changing dirty diapers or disciplining a teenager or waiting in line at the Motor Vehicles Office or working through a migraine headache or risking life and limb on the battlefield, "Why do I have to do this job?"

If you change one word, you change the whole Big Picture.

You also get the true question. It should be: "Why do I get to do this job?" Not "have to" but "get to."

Here is another answer: Count your blessings—literally.

Get a blank book, and write in it ten new things to be thankful for every day for a year—five from your life and five from the world. And don't forget meerkats. Three thousand six hundred fifty is really a very tiny number; both your life and your universe are much bigger than that.

These 3,650 things are gifts. Didn't anyone ever teach you to say "thank you" for gifts?

If you are wise enough, you will include even the sufferings that have made you wiser and stronger in the long run. In fact, that might very well include all of them, in the long run. For the run is very long.

Isn't the answer just to "let go"? We don't hear about "detachment" anymore.

Yes, we need detachment—detachment from our obsession with lesser things—but only for the sake of attachment to greater things. Detach to attach. Stop loving stupidly, but don't stop loving.

When you let something go, you sacrifice it for something else, for a reason. Keep your mind on that reason, that greater thing, not the thing you let go of. In other words, when you have to be negative, be positive. When you throw a thing away, don't throw your mind away, too, by gluing your mind to the thing you throw away.

You don't always have to give up second things for first things, but sometimes you do. The ultimate First Thing is God, or some quality of God: truth, goodness, or beauty.

There are reasons for letting go of good things and reasons for letting go of bad things, but the reasons are opposite. You let go of bad things because they're bad. It's like selling off a bad stock, or not making a bad bet. You let go of good things because there's something better. It's like buying a better stock or making a good bet.

What's the best bet in town?

Look it up: it's Pascal's wager.

Why do many people today say they are "spiritual" but not "religious"? What do they mean?

They mean one of three things: (1) that spirit is the only reality, which denies that God created the universe; or (2) that spirit is only good, which denies that there is such a thing as spiritual sin; or (3) that concrete, visible, institutional religion, especially the Catholic Church, is bad.

And in all three cases, what people are reacting most adamantly against is religious morality, especially sexual morality. Five institutional religious traditions—Roman Catholicism, Eastern Orthodoxy, Evangelical biblical Protestantism, Orthodox Judaism, and Islam—are the only forces left in the world that still oppose the sexual revolution and uphold the same principles of justice and charity and respect and piety and unselfishness and self-control when applied to sex as everyone holds everywhere else.

If you're religious, you probably believe that God issued a commandment that sex should not be adulterated. If you're spiritual, you probably think that's childish and that your spirituality is more adult. You're right—you like "adult" movies and "adult" bookstores. "Adult," in our culture, equals adulterated.

That's what it almost always comes down to.

Commandments always involve a yes and a no. These five traditions, from their beginnings, have always opposed sexual nos that everyone else supports: adultery, fornication, sodomy, contraception, pornography, and even masturbation.

That was not remarkable when most of the rest of the world agreed with it. Now almost nobody agrees with it, so we are accused of having a hang-up about sex. The sober are always accused of having a hang-up about alcoholism — by alcoholics.

And that's a war between two religions — two absolutes, not just two moralities. I never met anyone whose sexual rebellion was less than a nonnegotiable, noncompromising religious absolute. Always, they are people who are "living together" who happen to be Catholics, not Catholics who happen to be "living together"; or homosexuals who happen to be Jews, not Jews who happen to be homosexuals.

Spiritual warfare cannot be won except by spiritual weapons that are stronger than reason and rational morality. Those two things are terribly important; in fact, they are crucial to sanity for all individuals and cultures. But they have deeper roots that are spiritual, religious, and supernatural.

So, let us take the war to the enemy. They say they are "spiritual." Let us take them at their word. The source of their position is not mere biological passion. It is spiritual. And if the five traditions I listed above that oppose them are true, we know where these spirits come from.

"Let us take the war to the enemy" means not that our enemies are "spiritualists" but that our enemies are spirits. Our God-inspired guidebook tells us that "our wrestling is not against flesh and blood; but against principalities and power, against the rulers of the world of this darkness, against the spirits of wickedness in the high places" (Eph. 6:12, Douay-Rheims), who, having deceived their disciples, now try to deceive our whole world. Let us love these deceived disciples and our world by not loving or compromising with our true enemies.

Sin and Evil

Do you believe in Original Sin?

Oh boy, just what I always wanted to think about! Can't we think about nicer things, such as hemorrhoids, heart disease, taxes, and terrorism?

Yes, I do believe in Original Sin. Chesterton said that it's the only Christian dogma you can prove just by reading the daily newspaper.

But what does "Original Sin" mean? It's not what you do, or what your first ancestors did, but what you are. We sing because we're singers, and we sin because we're sinners.

Original Sin means that the whole world is (in the words of Pope Francis) a field hospital and everybody's injured, even the doctors and the nurses. So, who are the pop psychologists who tell you that you're not injured? They're the anesthesiologists.

If we didn't pop out of the womb as stupid, selfish idiots, we wouldn't have to correct ourselves and each other for the rest of our lives. There would be no moral struggle, no temptation. We wouldn't even have to socialize babies out of anything, or say no to anybody, not even to criminals.

Are we done yet?

Oh, no, it gets worse before it gets better. Original Sin means that we're all insane. What's more insane than choosing misery over joy? But that's what we do whenever we sin.

We know by experience that every time we choose God's way, which is unselfish love, we find joy: deep-down, long-range, ever-lasting joy. And every time we choose our own way over His, every time we sing Sinatra's song "I Did It My Way," every time we play God, we find misery and emptiness, deep down, long range, and lasting.

So what's our reaction to His next offer?

"Will you choose my right hand this time or my left hand? Joy or misery?"

How do we respond?

We say, "Well, God, you know, that's a difficult choice. It's a complex issue. Let's see. Let me try the left hand. Maybe it will work this time."

That's insanity. What's more insane than doing the same thing over and over again and thinking the result will be the opposite next time?

We have free will because God has two hands. God offers us choices between good and evil (most simply, between unselfishness and selfishness), because He's not the Godfather, who makes you an offer you can't refuse, but God the Father, who makes you an offer you *can* refuse, and often do. He offers joy and shows us the way to joy; and saints believe Him, and choose the way, and get the joy.

They say yes where we say no. That's why they're so much happier than we are.

So why don't we choose to be happy, unselfish saints instead of unhappy, selfish pigs?

Because we're insane.

So why does God love us? Why doesn't He just give up on us?

Because He's even more insane than we are, but in the opposite direction. That's the Good News.

He's crazy with love, and we're crazy without it.

What is your solution to the problem of evil?

First, let's distinguish three questions: the origin of evil, the answer to evil in practice, and the answer to evil in theory.

What is the origin of evil? Look in the mirror. The misuse of your own free will.

What is the answer to evil in practice? Jesus Christ. And the three things that glue you to Him are faith, hope, and charity.

The hardest question is the theoretical question: Why does God allow evil? The obvious answer is that He does this out of His wisdom and love. But how can that be?

It necessarily follows from God's goodness, power, and wisdom that all goods and all the evils of our lives, both physical and spiritual, are not outside, but inside, His plot, His plan.

If this is so, then wisdom would tell us to accept the physical goods and the physical evils, both the joys and the sorrows. Accept the joys joyfully (not sorrowfully: that's masochism) and the sorrows sorrowfully (not joyfully: that's masochism too). Try to accept the sufferings that He allows in your life even as your body and your instincts rightly rebel against them and try to escape them. But, of course, don't try to enjoy them: that's masochism.

"But I don't see what good could possibly be in this suffering or this frustration or this failure or this tragedy." That is the problem of evil. And the answer is really simple and obvious in theory and really hard to accept in practice. It's the answer God gave to Job: Of course you don't understand it.

You're not God. (Is that news to you?)

Evil is not good, and pain is not pleasant, and harm is not help. But good and pleasant and helpful things *can come from* bad and painful and harmful things. The Bible does not say that all things are good, just that God works all things together for good. You can't solve the problem of evil without looking at the Big Picture.

Are there some problems that are impossible to solve? For instance, how to reconcile justice and mercy?

No, not with God. "With God all things are possible" (see Mark 10:27).

Sometimes God solves impossible problems suddenly and immediately, as Jesus did to the cripple by the pool (John 5:2–9). Once each year, an angel touched the water of that pool, and the first person who got into the pool was miraculously healed. It happened every year. This poor guy was crippled, and so he had camped out beside the pool for years, hoping for his healing, but every time the angel came, he failed to be first in the pool. Why? Because he was crippled. Why did he need to get into the pool in the first place? Because he was crippled. Catch-22. Jesus solved that problem the same way Alexander the Great solved the puzzle of the Gordian knot. (Look it up.) He eliminated the middleman.

Whenever Jesus is confronted by an apparently unanswerable question or unsolvable problem, He solves it by not buying into the hidden assumption behind it, which is usually an either-or, a narrowing of possibilities. He finds a third possibility.

This is always the case when two goods apparently conflict. For instance, justice and mercy. Justice means giving others what they deserve, both in terms of rewards for good and in terms of punishments for evil. If there were no punishments for evil, rewards for good would lose their identity, just as if there were no rewards for good, punishments for evil would lose their identity.

But mercy seems to contradict justice. Mercy means *not* giving others the punishments they deserve. If a student flunks a final exam, which is announced as final and with no second chance for a retest, justice demands that he or she receive an F, but mercy demands something else.

Mercy is not just compassion or goodwill. Mercy is revocation of a punishment that is deserved. There is no mercy in Heaven because there is no need for mercy. But without mercy on earth — well, if we had no hope of mercy from God, we would all be hopeless and Hell-bound, for none of us *deserves* Heaven. And if we had no hope of mercy from men, how could we know what mercy is, and how could we believe it exists in God? And if we had no hope of mercy from men, quite apart from God, life would be unlivable.

But justice is absolute, and necessary. The psalms and the prophets are chock full of pleas to God from the righteous (David, Jeremiah, Moses) for justice. Unless God punishes the wicked and rewards the good, life is amoral.

But justice makes no room for mercy, and mercy is a contradiction to justice, for mercy says no to the punishments to which justice says yes.

But mercy cannot contradict justice because both are good. Only evil contradicts good.

Ultimately, no good thing can contradict or oppose any other good thing. Good and evil contradict each other and oppose each other and fight against each other, but not good and good. Somehow or other, the perspective under which two goods contradict each other has to be overcome, so that both goods are preserved and done greater, not less, justice to than they are under the perspective in which they contradict each other. Something higher has to find a way.

We often have dilemmas about justice and mercy, so it would be a very good thing if we learned how to deal with them in the best possible way, which is always God's way. How does He pull it off?

We know how He pulled it off in the biggest example of all: Christ's death and our salvation.

Let's look at what was behind that. What was His method? How did He do it?

The simplest answer is that God is love, and love always finds a way where nothing else can find a way.

But love is not "luv." It's a four-letter word, not a three-letter word. Love also has eyes. Jesus says, to the Jews who complain that they cannot understand His teaching, "If your will were to do the will of My Father, you would understand my teaching" (see John 7:17). Loving hearts use wise heads. Loving hearts *make* wise heads.

Here is how God did it: by the Incarnation. As Cardinal Newman wrote:

> O loving wisdom of our God!
> When all was sin and shame,
> A second Adam to the fight
> And to the rescue came.
>
> O wisest love, that flesh and blood,
> Which did in Adam fall,
> Should strive afresh against the foe,
> Should strive, and should prevail.

O generous love! That he who smote
In Man for man the foe,
The double agony in Man
For Man should undergo.

Psalm 85:10–11 prophesies how God will reconcile the "hard" demands of truth and justice and righteousness with the "soft" demands of mercy and peace: by Christ, in the Incarnation. Justice and peace (mercy) met together because Heaven and earth met together; justice sprang out of the earth, not just the heavens, and mercy sprang out of the heavens, and the divine nature (where it was not necessary or needed by God, but was given purely out of God's free choice), and not just out of the earth and human nature, where it is necessary and needed.

What is "the unforgivable sin"?

There must be one because the New Testament says so.

But God will forgive any sin if we truly repent. Jesus even forgave Judas. We are not capable of a sin that is greater than God's mercy. Our sin is like a speck of dirt, and His mercy is like the sea, in which sin disappears; His mercy washes away sin as a tidal wave washes away a feather.

Therefore, the only possible candidate for the unforgivable sin is impenitence, final impenitence, impenitent impenitence. God offers salvation for free, without price (Rev. 22:17); the only way not to get it is not to accept it. A gift, to be a gift, must be not only freely given but also freely received.

That is why pride is the greatest sin. Pride is not merely vanity or selfishness; it is the demand for autonomy, the demand to be independent of God. If that's what you want, that's what you will get. But the thing that you think is your Heaven is in fact really your Hell.

Morality

I read your friend Kirk Kilpatrick's book
Why Johnny Can't Tell Right from Wrong.
Tell us, please: What *is* right and wrong?

Right is right and wrong is wrong.

It's right to be right, and it's wrong to be wrong.

It's not wrong to be right, and it's not right to be wrong.

But if you think you're right, you're probably wrong, and if you think you're wrong, you're probably right.

If you're wrong, you can expect to be forgiven.

If you're right, you can expect to be punished.

Don't be afraid to say the *w*-word about yourself ("I was wrong") or the *r*-word about somebody else ("You're right").

Don't be "cool." Be honest.

And don't pretend you don't know the answer to that question you asked. You can't rip up your moral motherboard.

What do we do about imperfections?

Here's an answer that centers on the concept of imperfections as holes. It's from "Words Are Not Enough" by Alice Lok Cahana. It's about what the work of Heaven is in this world, and Alice learned it in the closest thing to Hell this world ever offered—namely, the death camp in Auschwitz. (Anthony Esolen says that in our time, torture chambers are more likely than universities to be places where we find God.)

> I made a painting that has holes in it. Why are there holes? Because God says to us, I cannot do all. I can create you but I cannot do it all. You have to help Me fix the holes and put everything together. This is the learning from the Holocaust. That each of us is there to fix the holes. My little brother, they put him in the crematorium. What did my mother, undressing in front of strangers, holding this little boy by the hand, what did she say to him? What? No one knows. *There* is a hole.

Alice also wrote of a Nazi who risked his life to give her a piece of edible bread: "So you see, everywhere there are good people, everywhere."

Do you think Dostoyevsky was right when
he said, "If God does not exist, everything is
permissible"? Does morality depend on religion?

Dostoyevsky was right ontologically but not epistemologically.
He was right ontologically because God is, in fact, the source and
standard of everything: being, truth, goodness, beauty. In objec-
tive fact, if God did not exist, not only morality but everything
else too, everything real, would not be real, because everything
real is relative to God, the absolute reality and the First Cause
of everything.

But we can know the effect without knowing the cause. We
can know the universe, which is the effect of God's creating it,
without knowing God. We can also know morality, which is a
reflection of God's nature as goodness, without knowing God.
Atheists have a conscience too. You can know morality without
knowing God just as you can know science without knowing
God. God is, in fact, the First Cause of all the truths about the
created universe that are known by science, but you don't have to
know God to know science. Science does not deduce the nature
of the universe from the nature of God; it works from the bottom, from the effects. Once you know God, however, you know
why the universe is so wise and beautiful. Ethics also does not

deduce what is good or evil, permissible or not, from the nature of God. Once you know God, however, you know the ultimate basis for morality.

Morality is based on God's nature. God says to His chosen people in Leviticus, the book of moral laws: "Be ye holy, because I the Lord your God am holy" (19:2, Douay-Rheims). To be morally good is to be real, because to be real is to be like God, the standard of reality, the Creator of all reality, and God is good. That is His nature, not just His will. His will follows His nature.

Morality is based on God's will only because His will expresses His nature. Morality is not based simply on God's will. It is not true that if God commanded us to hate instead of to love, then hate would be morally good and love morally evil. Morality is not arbitrary. And Dostoyevsky's saying did not mean to imply that it was. God's will is one with His reason, and His reason is one with His nature, His being. Moral laws are not just good but are also true, or reasonable, and "true" means "real," or "corresponding to reality."

This is denied by Fundamentalists, who deny the power of human reason to know God. It's also denied by voluntarists, who reduce mind to will, truth to goodness, and they say, too, with the Fundamentalists, that morality is all a matter of God's will, not His reason or His nature. There are Christian philosophers who are voluntarists: Scotus, Ockham, Descartes, Kierkegaard. But that is not mainline Christian theology. It is mainline Muslim theology ever since the Ash'arite fundamentalists won out in the ninth century.

There is a close practical connection between religion and morality. Every religion contains and teaches a high morality. Without religion, morality is on a much weaker foundation. And without morality, culture and civilization are on a much weaker foundation. Therefore, without religion, culture and civilization are much more insecure.

Practically speaking, religion has always been the strongest prop for morality. If you are alone on a dark street at night and you see a large, threatening-looking man coming toward you and carrying something under his arm, you naturally feel better when you see that it is a Bible.

Does God care more about truth
or goodness—about what we
believe or how we live?

I will answer that question if you answer this one: Does God care
more about men or women?

Cats or dogs? Sins of commission or sins of omission? Head
or heart?

Truth without love is cold; love without truth is blind. A
person without a mind is an animal. A person without a heart
is a computer.

The Devil loves to see us ask questions like "Which of these
two evils is less bad?" so that we don't feel so bad about doing
evil, and questions like "Which of these two goods is less good?"
so that we don't feel bad about ignoring good.

Philosophers tend to vacillate between rationalism and irrationalism. Rationalism puts down to second place the heart
and the will and morality, and irrationalism puts down to second
place the mind and truth. But both truth and goodness, truth
and love, are absolutes.

How can you do what is truly good unless you know truth?
And why seek truth unless it is good?

How can we be both just and merciful, both tough and tender, especially with our children?

Oops. If you hadn't added that last clause, I could have answered your question easily. God did it. Psalm 85:10–11 tells us how:

Mercy and truth are met together, justice and peace have kissed each other. Truth shall spring out of the earth and righteousness shall look down from heaven. (King James Version).

God reconciles truth and mercy by reconciling heaven and earth, by the Incarnation.

Now, how do we do that with our kids? We have to be both tough and tender, both true and merciful, both just and peaceful. And we do that with God's grace reaching down to us in Christ. Christ is the answer to how to raise good kids. The more He lives in us, the better we are at everything important, including parenting.

But it's not just a matter of following the rules in an instruction manual. Every day there are surprises, and each situation demands a new creative response. But the principles are the same, especially the one about truth and love, or justice and mercy: never compromise either one of them, whatever you do.

Speak the truth, but speak the truth in love. Love, but love truly and justly. A parent's job (and a politician's job too) is to find a way to incarnate love and truth, mercy and justice, in a world of selfishness and lies, so that truth can spring not only from eternal, universal, heavenly principles but also from changing, temporal, particular concrete situations. In other words, be faithful and be creative.

But how? There's no impersonal manual, but there is a perfect model. Christ was the most faithful man who ever lived, and He was also the most creative. The closer you get to Him, the more you will resemble him and find a way to be like him in both ways. But, of course, you will make a million mistakes. Repent. And never, never, never, never give up.

Suppose the Republican candidate is a liar, and a cheat, and a bully, and a bigot but pro-life, while the Democratic candidate is a nice person but pro-choice. How should I vote?

You'll never find either a perfect elephant or a perfect donkey. You have to judge which animal will do the most good and the least harm. "Politics" comes from "poly," which means "many," and "ticks," which are nasty little insect pests. Judge which boll weevil will infect the most cotton, and then choose the lesser of the two weevils.

You're not voting for an uncle. You're voting for a policymaker and a lawmaker. Vote for the one you think will do the most good and the least harm in the lives of 350 million Americans. And judge that good and harm by the standards of Catholic principles. That's what principles are for.

Good or harm where? In ordinary lives. By what standard? The hierarchy of goods—for instance, the three mentioned in a definite order in our founding documents: first life, then liberty, then the best conditions for the pursuit of happiness, including property and economics. Liberty comes before wealth and life before liberty because you can't pursue happiness if you are not free to do so, and you can't be free if you're dead. (Tyrants often offer you property only if you give up your liberty. They'd rather have your soul than your money.)

The right to life is the first good in ethics, as existence is the first good in metaphysics. So, if one candidate wants to decrease the murder of unborn babies, that trumps other things (with the exception of a nuclear war), even if he is personally a liar, an egotist, a narcissist, a Lothario, and a bully. In bridge, a trump card wins even if it's dirty. I said "if." The "if" is iffy. Your judgment call; that's the rule where government is of the people, by the people, and for the people. Of course, people are stupid, and sinful, and therefore so are their elected governments. So are kings. The best reason for preferring democracy over monarchy is not to give as many people as much power as possible but to give nobody too much power. Power corrupts. We all know that. So why do we pursue it?

My favorite presidential quote is from Harry Truman. He said, "In this great land of ours every single baby who is born an American citizen has an equal chance of someday becoming the President of the United States. That's just the chance the poor little bastard has to take in being born."

Politics is a business, and it's usually a dirty business. But it has to be done. It's like garbage collection. If you know somebody who wants to go to Georgetown to go into politics, congratulate him on going to garbage-collection school.

The Supernatural

Why don't we hear anything about angels anymore?

Because we don't want to.

They don't pop into and out of existence depending on whether we believe in them, but, on the other hand, they don't do much for us until they are asked and believed in.

Angels are not gods.

Nor are they human beings.

They are superior to us and inferior to God.

Almost all premodern cultures believed in something like angels, something between us and the Supreme Being. Sometimes these were mistakenly called gods. That was a mistake, but it was not a mistake to see human life as a kind of Jacob's Ladder, a stairway to Heaven; to believe in doors in the pitiless walls of the world, or better, doors in the sky, doors that sometimes opened. Today, for most of us "enlightened" people in Western civilization, those doors are locked.

Why are they locked?

Because Science can't discover them.

And the spectacular success of Science has convinced us that if Science can't detect it, it isn't real. (If you accepted the capital letter "S" in the word "science" in that sentence, you probably bought into that superstition, because what we create is not usually capitalized but what we believe creates us is.)

Science also can't detect beauty, love, or the self that knows all the things that Science knows. In other words, Science can't detect the scientist. The one thing that can't be one of the images on the screen of our consciousness is the thing that's projecting all the images. The subject of consciousness can't be simply one of the many objects of consciousness.

If science can't even detect our own spirit, mind, or consciousness, only its bodily instruments and effects, we can't expect it to detect angels, which are pure spirits without bodies.

Angels are persons without bodies; humans are persons with bodies. Angels are no more mythic than human persons are. Materialists say there are no such things as persons, souls, selves, egos, or spiritual substances, either human or angelic, because Science cannot detect them. They are at least consistent. If spirits outside bodies (angels) don't exist, then, for the same reasons, spirits inside bodies (human persons, selves, "I"s, egos, minds, or souls) don't exist either.

In fact, in a sense, spirits inside bodies, spirits that are the souls of bodies, are harder to believe in than spirits outside bodies. It's very strange that spirits should be joined to bodies. Whose weird idea was that? Probably the same One who designed the duck-billed platypus.

If angels are myths, then human persons are myths too. But if persons are myths, who invented them? If the answer is that we invented them, how can a myth be invented by another myth?

If there are no persons, but just bodies, then the attempt to find yourself is a bad knock-knock joke: Knock, knock. Who's there? Nobody. Nobody who? Nobody you.

Why don't we hear anything about angels anymore?

Probably, there is no irrefutable logical proof for the existence of angels outside of religious authorities, but there are all sorts of things that angels explain. Why did you suddenly, intuitively, jump back from stepping off the curb just as that car that you didn't see passed? And all those great ideas that seemed to pop into your mind without your planning them or willing them—where did they come from? And why is it that in every culture, many sane, wise, and reliable people (as well as many liars and kooks) claimed to have seen and interacted with angels? Why has every other culture except ours believed in something like angels? Were they just silly, like Elwood P. Dowd in *Harvey*, playing with an invisible rabbit friend even as an adult? In that case, let's all be atheists, because God is only the biggest invisible rabbit of all.

What difference do angels make?

For one thing, angels expand our mind. For another thing, they expand our lives. If there were no angels who interacted with us, no guardian angels who fought for us and protected us from temptations by evil spirits, we would be decimated by our true enemies, which are not flesh and blood but "principalities and powers of wickedness in high places." They are far more numerous, more intelligent, and more powerful than we are. Without help from superior friends, no one could survive that battle against superior enemies.

If you don't think there are superior enemies, do you honestly think that the evil you see in the souls of Hitler, Stalin, Pol Pot, and the Marquis de Sade is only human?

Your guardian angel protects you at every moment, even when you forget him completely. He does not need your remembering, your faith, your trust, your hope, or your love. But you do.

How long do acts of memory, faith, trust, hope, and love take? A few seconds. The old guardian angel prayer is a good one because it's short and simple and childlike:

> Angel of God, my guardian dear,
> To whom His love commits me here,
> Ever this day be at my side,
> To light and lead, to guard and guide.

Have you ever seen an angel?

No. But I have talked to people who have. And I have talked to Joan Webster Anderson, who strikes me as very sane and sober and reliable. She researched and wrote up a couple of books about people who saw angels, and unlike most such books, they seem to me quite reliable.

I'm not talking about the popular pictures of angels, e.g., with wings. Angels don't have wings because they don't have physical bodies. They are pure spirits. What do they look like? Like nothing. Or like whatever appearances they generate, either in matter or in our minds. They usually disguise themselves as human beings. They are much better at pretending to be humans than we are at pretending to be angels.

I have the impression that ghosts are more commonly seen than angels. I don't know why. Probably because angels are enablers, like Gandalf in *The Lord of the Rings*. They do most of their work invisibly. Like God, they appeal to faith more than to sight. They could use their great supernatural powers, as the Angel of Death did to the Egyptians in the Exodus, and to Sodom and Gomorrah, but that's not how God usually works, by sheer power. He gives us free choice. He doesn't bypass His creatures but works through them, both angels and humans.

When we get to Heaven, I think we will see our guardian angels, and God will show us all the millions of times they were guarding and guiding us, and inspiring us, and we will say, "Oh, so that was you all the time! Thank you."

If you cut out all the references to angels in the Bible, your scissors would wear out before you finished.

If angels do not exist, all the saints, all the bishops of the Church, and all orthodox Christians for two thousand years have been deceived, including Jesus Christ. In that case, Christianity is not a divine revelation at all. Angels are not the center of Christianity, but they are part of the "package deal."

The most practical thing in the Bible about angels for all of us is: "Do not neglect to show hospitality to strangers, for thereby some have entertainedl angels unawares" (Heb. 13:2).

Have you ever seen a ghost?

No, but I know some people who have, and I've read responsible, sober accounts of many more. Surprisingly, the Church has not settled the question of the existence of ghosts.

Personally, like the majority of people and the majority of intelligent people, I believe that after the body dies, the spirit lives on, so, in principle at least, I think there's a place for ghosts in the universe; ghosts are ontologically possible.

The Society for Psychical Research (there's one in England and one in America) has investigated many cases of ghosts appearing, with scientific exactness, but of course not with laboratory repeatability, so it's not hard science. The reason it can't be hard science is that ghosts are human souls whose bodies have died but they still have intelligence and will, so that whether, when, and where they appear is up to their will or, much more likely, God's will, and therefore it's not predictable or controllable, as any truly scientific experiment must be.

But the amount of credible anecdotal evidence for ghosts is massive. This makes their existence at least very probable and reasonable. There are probably many, many fakes and hallucinations as well as authentic ghost appearances, but that is what one would expect if ghosts did exist. Counterfeit money does not prove the nonexistence of real money; it almost presupposes it.

Of course, there is a lot of unscientific mythology. But there are not nearly that many even claimed appearances of pixies, elves, fairies, Bigfoot, the Loch Ness Monster, the Abominable Snowman, or little green men in flying saucers.

By the way, there is no credible example in all of human history of a ghost having physically harmed a living human being. Most ghosts seem weak and unhappy; they are probably working out their Purgatory. Don't fear them; pray for them.

Can a cat be possessed by a demon?

I don't know. Why do you ask? Until you answer that question, please do not invite me into your house.

By the way, I love cats as well as dogs. God invented both.

Have you ever seen a miracle?

Often. I see a miracle every time I go to Mass. And so do you.

I've also seen a physical miracle—a miraculous, or at least apparently miraculous and unexplainable, change in a brain tumor from being one kind of brain tumor (a malignant medulla blastoma) to a very different kind of tumor (a benign juvenile astrocytoma). I saw this because it happened to my daughter.

I have no scientific proof that it was a miracle, but because it happened after about a thousand people prayed for her, I doubt that it was just a lucky coincidence.

Imagine that you need a million dollars. You have nothing in your bank account. You know no one who is rich. One day, your bank tells you that someone deposited a million dollars in your account. Do you say, "Millions just happen"? Or do you look for someone to thank for it?

Perhaps my daughter's healing was not a miracle. Perhaps such a sudden change in a tumor, from one kind to a very different kind, is statistically just barely possible. Perhaps there is a very tiny statistical chance of that happening, by natural forces that we do not understand. In that case, there is no one to thank for it.

And perhaps life can appear on some planet in this universe if all the conditions are just right—if the temperature of the primeval fireball a millionth of a second after the Big Bang was not a millionth of a degree hotter or a millionth of a degree colder so that, through that tiny window of opportunity, the carbon atom, the basis of all life, could form. And perhaps evolution could happen on this planet if the sun is just far enough away so that it's not too hot or too cold and the moon is just far enough away to make the tides so that life can evolve in the sea and move to land, and the sun's rays hit the primeval earth at just the right distance and intensity to evolve protein molecules. Perhaps all these trillions and trillions of tiny windows of opportunity all happened to open right, and it's all chance, in which case there's no one to thank for our being here.

And perhaps the million dollars just happened to appear in your bank account because of a computer mistake. It's possible. In which case, there is no one to thank for it.

If you are an atheist and you believe that, I'm so sorry for you. You have freely chosen to deprive yourself of the first source of wisdom and happiness, which is gratitude.

Heaven

What will Heaven be like?

Heaven will be like everything good and beautiful on earth but more so. Like marriage compared with courtship, like the main course compared with an appetizer, like the world's best wine compared with vinegar.

It will be ridiculously better than anything we can imagine. If you can imagine it, it's not Heaven. That's the Bible's answer: "Eye has not seen, ear has not heard, nor has it entered into the heart of man, the things God has prepared for those who love Him" (see 1 Cor. 2:9).

It's a surprise, and therefore it's not just peace and contentment and happiness but also joy and excitement and wonder—something that never gets boring. It's falling more and more in love with the God who is more beautiful than anything you ever imagined and will be more beautiful every time we look at Him.

Why is that true?

Why isn't that just dreaming and wishful thinking?

Because God loves us and wants to give us maximum joy, and knows how, and can, and will. If all of that's not true, we have no hope; if God hates us, or if God is a Scrooge with His gifts, or if God is stupid, or weak, or doesn't care, then God isn't God, and if even God isn't God, then there is no God.

What do you think you will do in Heaven? Will
you just sit in church and smile all the time?

The most profound and brilliant philosopher I ever knew, Fr.
Norris Clarke, S.J., gave a talk about life after death and what
each of us would do in Heaven. He was in his nineties. During
the question-and-answer period, I asked him what he personally
hoped to do in Heaven. He answered, "I hope to design strange
fish."

I know of no philosopher who would give a more memorable
answer than that.

Fr. Clarke's answer is shockingly good because it is concrete
and personal. Another kind of answer, not quite so shockingly
good, is also good because it is universal. Here it is.

Remember the most joyful, ecstatic, self-forgetful experience
you ever had. That was a tiny appetizer or foretaste of what you
are designed for.

Heaven exceeds all that we can imagine or conceive. It is an
infinite, incomprehensible, inconceivable, incredible, ineffable,
inexhaustible, infallible, indestructible, invulnerable ecstasy; an
unpredictable, unfathomable, unthinkable, unspeakable, unimaginable, undiminished, uninterrupted, unending, unwavering,
untiring, unquenchable, untamed, untainted, unadulterated,

unashamed orgasm of our spirit perpetually penetrated by pure and perfect Love.

If we experienced even a moment of that now, we would just disappear like a flea in a solar flare. We would die of delight. That's why we are down here in the shadowlands: it is a thickening process.

How many people do you think will be in Heaven?

I think the number will be more than you think and also less than you think. That's the only thing Jesus ever said about it: "Many of the first shall be last and the last shall be first."

When His disciples asked him, "Lord, will many be saved?" they were probably thinking something like this: We'd like to know the comparative population statistics of Heaven and Hell, and if anybody knows, He does, so let's get His answer before it's too late. If He says 10 percent go to Heaven, we'll sweat, and if he says 90 percent, we'll relax, and if he says 50 percent, we'll be confused, but at least we'll know our chances."

His answer: "Strive to enter in" (see Luke 13:23–24).

The answer is in practice, not in theory. The population of Heaven is up to each one of us. No one ever goes to either place without his own free choice.

Our ancestors tended to think that the vast majority didn't make it. Our generation tends to think that everybody, or nearly everybody, makes it to Heaven. Both are wrong, not because the answer is wrong but because the question is wrong.

Jesus often does that. Instead of answering the question, He answers the answerer by questioning the question.

What language will we speak in Heaven?

Two: silent adoration and music. In Heaven, whatever is not silence is music, and whatever is not music is silence. Hell is perpetual loud bragging and shouting against a background of unending "Christian rock." Or something worse, something "eye has not seen, ear has not heard, nor has it entered into the heart of man."

Music is the universal language. We dimly intuit that it is the most profound of all the arts, and yet it is the least intelligible, least explainable one. The only adequate explanation for that paradox is that it is Heaven's language. That explains both its profundity and its mystery.

Or you could argue that Hebrew is Heaven's language because a baby's first word is naturally the Hebrew word for God, "Ab-ba," which means "Daddy." Look at the expression on the face of a baby who is being held by his mother or father and is looking up into his parent's eyes and smiling. What you see there is the essence of religion, which is simple trust, and joyful surrender, and the peace that comes with that surrender, which is the meaning of the Hebrew word "shalom" and the Arabic word "islam." In that look on the baby's face you can see the oneness of faith, hope, and love.

That's still in us, by nature. To believe in God is also to believe in yourself, in your deepest, most primal instincts.

I'm not sure I want to go to Heaven, because I find prayer difficult and not rewarding most of the time, and I'm bored and distracted most of the time in church, and I'm just not a contemplative. The Beatific Vision is not something I look forward to, even though I believe all that the Church teaches with my mind and I accept it with my will, but it doesn't touch my heart much at all.

Thank you very, very much for being so honest. I felt exactly the same way as you did when I was younger, and sometimes I still do, and I'm almost certain there are dozens of persons reading this book who are very, very pleased, surprised, and grateful to you for saying what they feel too but haven't dared to say.

Three answers. First, thank God that you believe and accept the whole divinely revealed shebang with your mind and will, even though your heart is not there, even though you do not have what the saints call "sensible consolations." That act of faith on your part is especially precious to God because it's not easy. Jesus on the Cross did not feel great "sensible consolations" either. He prayed, "My God, my God, why hast thou forsaken me?" (Matt. 27:46). Your faith and hope and charity when they are still alive in that state of the "dark night" are far more powerful and worth more than deep positive emotions. All the saints say that: that emotions, even though they are powerful, are not as important as we think. We modern Americans are too much into pop psychology. The saints are not. They're into something much more serious and solid and eternal.

Second, you probably have ADD. Many intelligent people do. That's why they get bored so easily and are so distractible. It's a handicap, but it is also God's gift to you. He knows what He is doing.

Third, I felt the same way you did, and I had a kind of crisis because I didn't want to go to Heaven and sit in an eternal church service, but I didn't want to go to the other place, and I knew I couldn't stay here forever. What resolved my problem was the verse in Revelation that says that there is no temple in Heaven because God is there (21:22). God is interesting. Proof of that is Jesus, the most perfect and complete revelation of God that we ever had or ever will have. Jesus is the only man in history who never bored anybody who ever met Him.

So just keep your hand to the plow and march on. God does not command us to feel anything, and He is in command of whatever feelings we get.

He knows what He is doing.

Just trust and obey. Nothing else matters.

Why don't Catholics believe in reincarnation?

1. The Bible contradicts it: "It is appointed unto men once to die, and after this the judgment" (Heb. 9:27).

2. The Church has always denied it, especially when it was popular in the surrounding non-Christian culture, e.g., in ancient Greece.

3. Reincarnation insults the body. It's Cartesian, or Platonic, or Gnostic. It locates our whole humanity in the soul or spirit and treats the body merely as our temporary motel room at best and as a tomb or prison at worst. (In Greek, the word for "body," *soma*, is almost the same as the word for "tomb," *sema*.) The Jewish and Christian Scriptures tell us that God invented and created the body, and that the image of God is bodily as well as spiritual. The first time "the image of God" is mentioned, in Genesis 2:7, it is identified as "male and female." The words mean physical, biological male and female, not just masculine and feminine minds.

By the way, reincarnation makes the same mistake as contraception: it reduces the body to an object, a thing. It's no longer a part of me; it's a part of the world out there.

In Platonic philosophy, life after death consists of being free from the body. In Judaism and Christianity and Islam, it consists in the resurrection of the body. The resurrected Christ had a physical body that was touched, and that ate food, precisely to prove that it was *not* a ghost, a pure spirit.

Neo-Platonism and the Gnosticism that was based on it went a step further than Plato and declared that the body was the cause of all sin and evil. A convenient philosophy for sinners: "My body made me do it. It's Your fault, God, for giving me this albatross around my spirit's neck."

Descartes was a Catholic, at least nominally, so he did not believe either of those two heresies, but he did believe that the body was a separate and distinct substance or thing or entity from the soul. Bodies had space but no thought; minds had thought but no space; so there was nothing common to them to unite them. We are essentially only minds, ghosts haunting the houses of our bodies. A most unrealistic and unhealthy psychology. Reincarnation, like Cartesian dualism, treats bodies as external temporary dwelling places.

The first Christian philosopher, Justin Martyr, was a Platonist, and he met a Christian who asked him how he, as a Platonist, explained why bodies existed. Justin answered that they were punishments given by the gods, just punishments for sins committed in some previous bodily life. Justin was asked how he knew or remembered his previous lives, and the answer was that he didn't. "So how could you be punished and rehabilitated and improved if you did not remember your crimes?" And then the Christian asked Justin what was his hope as a Platonist, and Justin answered that it was freedom from all bodies in Heaven once the punishments and rehabilitations were complete after enough reincarnations on earth. But the Christian asked: Is this purely spiritual Heaven perfect? And the answer was yes.

Why? Because there are no bodies there. But if it's perfect, there's no sin. So how are the gods just for punishing us by putting us into bodies if we didn't sin in Heaven? In other words, in the Platonic scheme of reincarnation, the beginning of bodies (punishment for sin) and the end of bodies (freedom from bodies in Heaven) contradict each other. Justin could not answer that question. He soon became a Christian and realized that this new faith was also a more rational philosophy.

4. Reincarnation takes the gusto and drama out of life. If you get infinite retests until you pass, there's no drama to the test. There's drama in life because you get only one chance. As the old commercial said, "You go around only once in life, so grab the gusto." That commercial would be censored today; it contradicts and offends those who believe in reincarnation.

5. Reincarnation almost always goes together with pantheism. To explain why, we need some philosophy. It's matter that individuates any one essential form, that multiplies a species into many members. We all have the same essential form or essence—namely, human nature—as all copies of a certain book have the same essential form; but we are many, as there are many copies of the book, in quantity, because of matter, not form. The form is one; the matter is many. There are many material copies of the same essential form. So, if we are one in spirit and many only in matter (that's premise one), and if we are essentially only spirit (that's premise two for those who believe in reincarnation), then the logical conclusion is that we are essentially only one being, not many beings. We are all waves of the divine sea, all parts of God. That's pantheism.

6. Reincarnation insults individuality. With reincarnation, your life is not unique. You were once somebody else. Your unique you, your "I," is relative and exchangeable, like a mask or a uniform.

7. There is no good argument or evidence for reincarnation. Apparent evidence such as memories from past lives that have

been empirically confirmed (the location of hidden treasures, for example) can all be explained in other ways, either by secret information leaked by other living human beings, or as mental telepathy by evil spirits who want to deceive us. (And I challenge anyone who thinks that that idea is ridiculous or disprovable to a debate on the reality of telepathy, of spirits, of evil spirits, and of evil—four assumptions that materialists typically deny).

Science

Is there a multiverse?

Atheist scientists try to avoid the implications of the truth of the "singularity" of the Big Bang (i.e., the claim that all the matter, time, and space in the universe has a single origin and cause, which they desperately want to avoid calling "God"), so they posit a "multiverse." Our universe, they say, is only one of many.

There is not a scrap of scientific evidence for the existence of any other universe. (Actually, it is theology that makes it possible: the God who freely created this universe, not in time but in eternity, could have created others, with their own time and matter and space, just as a single author can write many books.)

Other universes are only theoretically possible, both scientifically and theologically, i.e., the idea is not logically self-contradictory and meaningless.

On the other hand, there *is* evidence of other universes. There are over seven billion other universes in existence. Every human mind lives in its own universe, in a sense, even while living in this common universe. When you sit and I stand, my universe has you "down there" but your universe has you "up here." In your universe, you are the one subject or knower, and I am one of many objects known; in my universe, I am the one knowing subject and you are one of many objects known.

So, there is an actual multiverse. But everything in it—all seven-plus billion universes—depends on the one Big Bang.

And if there is a Big Bang, there must be a Big Banger. Whether you use the word "God" or not, and whether you identify it with the God of the Bible, it must exist, unless something can come from absolutely nothing. And if you believe that, I have a time-share in Florida that I will sell you. (Years ago, I got it from this sucker in exchange for the Brooklyn Bridge, which I told him I owned. It was a scam: the guy I sold the bridge to doesn't have to pay upkeep and taxes on it.)

Why is there a war between science and religion? How did it begin?

Have you stopped planning terrorist attacks yet?

When did you begin?

That's what logicians call a "complex question" or a "question-begging question," a question that has a hidden assumption.

And the assumption is false. There is no such war. It is a myth.

Proof of that is the fact that not a single doctrine of religion—of the Christian religion, anyway—has ever been disproved by a single discovery of any science at any time in the history of the world.

If you deny that, tell me: Which doctrine, which orthodox understanding of which doctrine, has been disproved by which discovery of which science or which scientist, when and where?

Nobody has ever been able to answer that question. Anyone who speaks of the so-called war between science and religion always talks about science in general and religion in general, as abstractions.

God invented the universe and also the human mind, and He also invented true religion. He made these three things always to correspond. A story always has a setting, characters, a plot, and a theme. These four dimensions contradict each other only if the author is schizophrenic. The universe is the setting, and we are the characters, and history is the plot, and religion is the theme of the story.

Science is simply our minds' discovering the nature of the universe. Of the four dimensions, it is the least important. It is relative to the other three; it is the setting for the other three.

What apparent but not real contradictions exist between science and religion that explain that false idea? Paleontology really does contradict the idea that many religious people have that the earth is only six thousand years old. But that's not religion; that's misunderstanding of symbolic language. Creation does not contradict evolution. The idea that God does not use natural causes but miraculously creates each species out of nothing contradicts evolution, but that's not religion; in fact, that even contradicts what Genesis says. After God says "let there be" the universe, He says "let the earth bring forth" and "let the waters bring forth" different species. And even the order of creation in Genesis is the same as the order of evolution, from nonliving to living, from simple to complex, and from subrational to rational. (That's why woman was made after man: man is not quite as rational as woman. Proof of that is the fact that he thinks he is more rational than woman.)

There have indeed been intellectual wars between some religious believers and some scientists—for instance, between the stubborn bishops who refused to look through Galileo's telescope and Galileo, who refused to call his hypothesis only a hypothesis before it was proved. By the way, the pope supported and financed Galileo, and Copernicus, who had the same correct idea, was a priest who had no trouble with the Church. The inventor of Big Bang cosmology was also a priest. The two greatest scientists of all time, Newton and Einstein, were theists, or deists, but not atheists.

Why is there a war between science and religion?

Religion and science support each other. Religion explains why science works. The universe is like a very large book, or a computer. Religion explains why it's so intelligible: because it was invented by intelligence; it did not come about by blind, random chance. (Intelligence sometimes designs chance and randomness, as in gambling casinos, but mere chance cannot design intelligence.) And science supports religion.

Religion, especially Christianity, makes many claims that science can investigate. For instance, if science discovered the bones of the dead Jesus, it would disprove Christianity. Christianity is a historical religion, and vulnerable to scientific discoveries. But it has never been disproved.

Books and Music

What do you love most about the Bible?

I love its nouns.

The Bible is great, and heavy, and big, and important, because of its nouns.

Even if we don't understand them much, we know such words are like hundred-car freight trains freighted with meaning: they are mountains; they are oceans; they are supernovas. God, Man, Woman, Life, Death, Love, Hate, Goodness, Evil, Justice, Word, Spirit, Father, Mother, Son, Daughter, Brother, Sister, Light, Water, Earth, Sky, Sun, Moon, Name, War, Peace.

You just know that whatever else those words are, those are Great Beasts.

I even love the parts most people love the least, the genealogies. Those are people. Every one of them is just as real and just as important as you are.

If you could take only ten books with
you to a desert island for the rest of
your life, what would they be?

Do I get to include the whole Bible?

Yes.

Then I also get to include other anthologies, such as the complete works of Plato and C.S. Lewis and G.K. Chesterton and
Shakespeare. Gotcha! So here they are. The complete works of
each of the following authors:

God (the Bible)
Augustine
Aquinas
Tolkien
C.S. Lewis
G.K. Chesterton
Shakespeare
St. John of the Cross
Dostoyevsky
Plato

*Suppose you could have only one book from each of these authors
instead of anthologies. What single volumes would you choose?*

John's Gospel
Augustine's *Confessions*
Aquinas's *Summa Theologiae*
Tolkien's *Lord of the Rings*
Lewis's *Chronicles of Narnia* (if that counts as seven
  instead of one, make it *Till We Have Faces*)
Chesterton's *Orthodoxy*
Shakespeare's *Hamlet*
St. John of the Cross's *Ascent of Mount Carmel*
Dostoyevsky's *The Brothers Karamazov*
Let me exchange Plato for Pascal's *Pensées*.

Give us some other individual titles to read on the beach.

Gladly. This is all very personal, you understand: these are
the ones that gave me the most joy.
 Plato's *Apology, Gorgias, Phaedo,* and *Republic*
 Chesterton's *The Everlasting Man* and *The Man Who*
  Was Thursday and his poem *Lepanto*
 Lewis's *Mere Christianity, The Problem of Pain, The*
  Great Divorce, and *The Screwtape Letters*
 Tolstoy's *Confession, War and Peace,* and *The Death of*
  Ivan Ilych
 Shakespeare's other tragedies: *King Lear, Macbeth,* and
  Julius Caesar; and *A Midsummer Night's Dream,* his
  most comical comedy
 Aristotle's *Nicomachean Ethics*
 Anselm's *Proslogium*
 Boethius's *The Consolation of Philosophy*
 Homer's *Iliad* and *Odyssey*
 Dante's *Divine Comedy*

If you could take only ten books with you to a desert island . . .

Walter M. Miller's *A Canticle for Leibowitz*, the greatest
  of all science fiction novels
Walker Percy's *Lost in the Cosmos*, the funniest phi-
  losophy book ever written
Sheldon Vanauken's *A Severe Mercy*, and I guarantee
  you will weep
Brother Lawrence's *The Practice of the Presence of God*,
  the easiest book on how to be a saint
Jean-Pierre de Caussade's *Abandonment to Divine
  Providence*
Charles Williams's *Descent into Hell*, the scariest book
  I've ever read
Thornton Wilder's *Our Town*, the most performed
  play in the world
Samuel Beckett's *Waiting for Godot*, the funniest play
  in the world
Hemingway's *The Old Man and the Sea*
Michael O'Brien novels, especially *Father Elijah* and
  Strangers and Sojourners
Dickens's *A Tale of Two Cities*

Suppose you could take only one book.

If I couldn't have any of the others, I'd probably pick *How
to Build a Boat*.

I'd probably drown in the attempt to sail it, but life without
books is barely worth living.

Erasmus said, "When I have a little extra money, I buy books,
and if there's money left over, I buy food." Reading great books is
like having a conversation with the ghosts of the greatest minds
who ever lived.

Can fiction be true or false?

Yes. There are true and false stories both in fiction and in real life. Stories are mankind's oldest and most universal art. Every group of humans tells stories, especially about themselves and people like them.

Stories are either true or false—truths or lies about people and about life.

The most important truth stories can tell is that there is hope, that there is meaning to life.

Most modern stories imply that this is an illusion created by us. That is why most modern stories are false, are lies. They are also boring and depressing. And that is also why *The Lord of the Rings* is so powerful and healing: because it is true.

Another common lie about life, and about stories, is that there is no such thing as a soul, or free will, or an absolute morality, or salvation and damnation. Stories that assume that lie are never as interesting as stories that assume the opposite, for nothing is more interesting, more dramatic, and more important than whether a soul will go to Heaven or to Hell. No merely temporary and physical pleasure, however ecstatic, and no suffering, however horrendous, is even interesting, much less compelling, compared with that.

That is why most people today are bored. The very word "boredom" did not exist in ancient cultures and languages.

Only people who have lost their humanity and who believe they are just clever animals, and are trying to live like happy animals, or are on their way to becoming mere animals—only such fools can be bored.

You've written more than eighty books.
Which of them is your favorite?

That depends on what I favor it for.

If you ask which book took the most time and work and sweat and revision, and the one that has the most different parts of me in it, it's my novel *An Ocean Full of Angels*, which is an angel's eye view of the connection between Jesus Christ, dead Vikings, philosophical Muslims, Russian prophets, the superiority of islands, the Great Blizzard of '78, two and a half popes in one year, armless nature, mystics, the legend of the Wandering Jew, the demon Hurricano, the disguises of angels, the dooms of the Boston Red Sox, the Sea Serpent, the Palestinian "intifada," the sexual revolution, post-abortion trauma, Romeo and Juliet, Jewish mother substitutes, the psychology of suicide, home-baked bread, the Theory of Everything, Dutch Calvinist seminarians, humanity's obsession with the sea, sassy Black feminists, the identity crisis of Catholic universities, Caribbean rubber dancers, false Messiahs, the mysticism of body surfing, and the end of the world. But that's an oversimplification.

If you ask which book I'd make everybody in the world read if I could, it's *Jesus Shock*.

If you ask which book is the best written, I think it's *Christianity for Modern Pagans: Pascal's Pensées*, because Pascal is such a good writer.

If you ask which book is the most philosophical, it's *Summa of the Summa*, which is the most philosophically important passages in Aquinas's *Summa Theologiae*, edited and footnoted and explained.

If you ask which book is the closest to my heart, it's either *Heaven, the Heart's Deepest Longing* or *I Burned for Your Peace*, which is about Augustine's *Confessions*, or the new one on the heart, *The Highways of the Heart*.

If you ask which book I'd give to a materialist and naturalist and atheist who is open minded, it's *Doors in the Walls of the World*.

The one that most students will read and learn philosophy from is probably my four-volume history of philosophy for beginners, *Socrates' Children: The 100 Greatest Philosophers*.

You quote Chesterton a lot. Tell us one practical thing you've learned from Chesterton.

Gladly. I learned Mooreeffoc.

It's an exotic-sounding word. It's simply "coffee room" backward, as seen from the inside of the door of a coffee room. G. K. Chesterton uses it as an image for the kind of mental fantasy that anyone can indulge in without expense or travel or danger. Just look at familiar things in an unfamiliar way: backward, or upside down, or from an angle. Tilt your head to one side, and the whole world looks new, and weird, and adventurous.

Chesterton defines an adventure as "nothing but an inconvenience rightly considered." An inconvenience is "nothing but an adventure wrongly considered."

During World War II, meat was scarce and tough in England. Parents made it more edible for their kids by saying it was mastodon meat killed by a caveman, or dinosaur meat secured by a time traveler. By dipping it in fantasy, you make it wonderful. But (and here is the real point) you can see all ordinary things as new and wonderful by dipping them in fantasy.

Thus, in a fantasy such as *The Lord of the Rings*, it is not just the wizards and orcs and elves and dwarves but the ordinary things — the hobbits themselves and their food and the trees and the roads they travel — that are enchanted and made wonderful by being dipped (incorporated) in fantasy. We do not have orcs and elves, but we do have bread and trees. Dip them in fantasy and you see them truly. For everything really is wonderful and ceases to be so only when we let layers of the dust of familiarity accumulate on them. Fantasy blows away that dust.

Children understand this best. Don't lose your childhood. You are not a train moving down the track of progress and leaving each station behind as you move to the next one; you are a snowball rolling downhill, keeping the snow you picked up at the beginning of your journey, at the top of the hill, inside you, nearest to your heart, as you roll down the hill.

Samuel Johnson said, when he was fat and fifty, that one of the greatest pleasures of his life was rolling down a hill full of snow. He had added to himself more of two things at the bottom than at the top: snow and happiness.

What are your favorite movies?

Here's an extended list.

The Passion of the Christ
A Man for All Seasons
Monty Python and the Holy Grail (comedy)
Dr. Strangelove (comedy)
A Fish Called Wanda (comedy)
Gone with the Wind
Casablanca
E.T.
Mrs. Doubtfire (comedy)
Tootsie (comedy)
Saving Private Ryan
The Shawshank Redemption
Dead Man Walking
The Lord of the Rings
Shadowlands
Hamlet (Mel Gibson version)
Star Wars (the original)
The Godfather: Part II
Life Is Beautiful
The Last of the Mohicans (Daniel Day-Lewis version)
The Untouchables

Rain Man
The Mission
Endless Summer
The Princess Bride (comedy)
The Seventh Seal
Vertigo
The Prisoner (with Alec Guinness)
The Eye of the Needle
High Noon
To Kill a Mockingbird
Schindler's List
Inglourious Basterds (comedy)
My Favorite Year (comedy)
The African Queen
Liar, Liar (comedy)
North Shore
Harry Potter (the original)
Pride and Prejudice
Pirates of the Caribbean (the original) (comedy)
Indiana Jones and the Temple of Doom
Galaxy Quest (comedy)
My Cousin Vinny (comedy)
Somewhere in Time
Cannery Row (comedy)
In the Way of the Black Raven (Icelandic)
The Red Balloon
Spirited Away
Silence (Martin Scorsese)
The Three Kings
Midnight Run (comedy)
Henry V

What are your favorite movies?

Dr. Zhivago
Love and Death (comedy)
The Natural
The Exorcist
Howard's End
Clue (comedy)
The Remains of the Day
Bull Durham (comedy)
The Gods Must be Crazy (comedy)
Dracula (Frank Longello)
The Sunset Limited
Equus

What do you think about Christian rock — contemporary Christian music?

I don't think anything about it, because it makes me stop thinking and makes me start grimacing with embarrassment and mental pain. And I don't think those who love it think anything about it either because it does to thinking what cavities do to teeth.

It is shallow, stupid, self-absorbed, sentimental, sissy, silly, sappy, soupy, and smarmy. It is fit only for Southern California teeny-boppers or for those who are so hokey and pokey that they think the hokey-pokey really is "what it's all about."

"Christian rock" is a deep insult not only to Christianity but to rock.

Comparing those so-called praise choruses to the great old classic Christian hymns is like comparing maggots to lions, mayflies to eagles, or a fat, big-mouthed drunk with St. Vitus dance hopping on hot coals to the Bolshoi Ballet. The other kind of contemporary worship music, more popular in Catholic churches now, much of it from the St. Louis Jesuits, sounds like the music that would come from a pansy imitating a kitten, or a brain made of limp noodles, or a pastel yellow happy face on pot.

It is not a question of personal taste or even aesthetics. It's a question of theology. Music is a sign. It points to something. It points to Christ. The Church's Christ is Christ the King. The Christ of today's popular liturgical music is Christ the Kitten.

Now ask me how I *really* feel about it.

There's a medieval story about a king who had to choose between supporting Rome or Byzantium. He sampled both liturgies, and said, "The Orthodox liturgy brings me to Heaven. I hear angels there. I choose Heaven for my kingdom."

There are many liturgies like that. Here is a prayer from the Chaldean liturgy. Compare it with "contemporary Christian" music:

> Before the glorious seat of Thy majesty, O Lord, and the awful judgment seat of Thy burning love, and the absolving altar which Thy command hath set up, and the place where Thy glory dwelleth, we Thy people and the sheep of Thy fold do kneel with thousands of the cherubim, singing Alleluia, and many times ten thousand seraphim and archangels, acclaiming Thy holiness, worshipping, confessing, and praising Thee at all time, O Lord of all.

I'm not saying you should choose a church based on liturgy alone. Doctrinal truth has to come first, and then holiness: Does it teach and practice sanctity? And the historical link with Christ is crucial: Is this the one, holy, catholic, and apostolic Church that He founded? But liturgy is important too, because it is a sacramental sign that effects what it signifies, and it usually points to and goes with those two other things. You see the presence of the same Christ in the Church's truth, in her goodness, and in her beauty.

Culture

You write about fighting the "culture wars." Why are you countercultural?

Because of the lies our popular culture tells us. Here are some of them:

- You are the most important person in the whole wide world.
- You have a right to happiness.
- The old idea that men and women are different in nature is "sexism."
- Whom you vote for is more important than who your friends are.
- Love is a feeling.
- The worst sin in the world is not being politically correct.
- The reason to go to college is to get a good job.
- Silence is boring.
- Nature is boring.
- Church is boring.
- Babies are boring.
- Motherhood is boring.
- Prayer is boring.
- Economics is not boring.

- Getting drunk is not boring.
- Humility is for suckers.
- You need a lot of "friends."
- Sex is for fun. Sons and daughters are "accidents."
- You can't live without it.
- America is the hope for the rest of the world.
- America is hopelessly corrupt.
- Primitives are primitive.
- It's a woman's right to kill her son or daughter in the womb. But not outside it.
- You can be whatever you want to be.
- Death is morbid.
- Technology makes us powerful.
- Be your own best friend.
- Truth is relative.
- Religion confines you; "spirituality" expands you.
- Elephants and donkeys can never cooperate.

Which technological invention do you think is the most dangerous?

Wow, that is a really thoughtful question. My first answer is the *nuclear bomb* because that made possible the total suicide of the entire human race for the first time. But I think our survival instinct is strong enough to make it likely that that won't happen, despite the fact that humans can always outdo our expectations in wickedness.

So, I'll look for a better answer. My next candidate would be the *Pill* (the only medication in history whose name is simply "the"). The contraceptive made the sexual revolution possible, and that changed pregnancy into a disease and children into accidents. That is the most revolutionary revolution since Christianity because it is in fact undermining and eventually destroying the one and only institution that is absolutely necessary for human morality and happiness — namely, the family — and sending us straight to Brave New World. Where else do we learn morality's most important lesson — namely, that we are to love and be loved not for what we can accomplish, which is what happens in the workplace and in public, but simply for existing. Only the family loves you that way. Subtract that, and you may get a world of peace and prosperity and contentment, but it is not human. It is not a family; it is a factory. So, I would go as far as to say that Pope Paul VI was a prophet and that *Humanae Vitae* was the most socially important encyclical of all time. It's also by far the one encyclical that is more hated and disobeyed by Catholics than any other in two thousand years.

A third possible answer is the *clock*, because that made it possible for people to live in a new kind of time — artificial, man-made, or man-defined time instead of natural time. Time influences absolutely everything in life. So I think the clock has changed more of life than any other invention.

A fourth answer is one that has appeared only in the last generation. It is the thing that nearly everyone under thirty is the most addicted to: more than to sex or alcohol or drugs. It's the *smartphone*. That little gray machine with the apple on it, the apple with a bite taken out of it — where did it come from? Who made it and why? How bold is its label! It has a signature on it that tells you who its very clever inventor is. It comes with a warning: take a bite of this apple, and you will fall from Love to Power, from Happiness to Success, from Wisdom to Knowledge, and from Freedom to Addiction.

I give my students the option of writing an original extra-credit essay on "How my world and my life were different during the 24 hours during which I looked at no screen: smartphone, computer, tablet, Kindle, TV, etc., and just looked at the world and other people." So far, eight out of ten have confessed that they tried and thought they could do it but couldn't. They could not live for twenty-four hours without their iPhone.

Even crack cocaine addicts can sometimes live for twenty-four hours without crack. And they don't get academic credit for it.

Perhaps this is the most widespread addiction in the history of the world: the substitution of the artificial world, the digital world, for the real world. It might even end the human race, if digital pornography replaces real sex completely.

Are you an optimist or a pessimist about our culture?

Chesterton says that when he was a little boy, he thought there were two kinds of "doctors of philosophy": optimists and pessimists. Optimists looked after your eyes and pessimists looked after your feet. That's about right. Optimists look up and find all sorts of things to be optimistic about, and pessimists look down and find all sorts of things to be pessimistic about. There have always been both kinds, and they have always been both right and wrong.

Optimism and pessimism are either emotions or ideologies. As a Christian, I live by neither emotion nor by ideology but by divine revelation, which tells me both that "the heart of man is desperately wicked" (see Jer. 17:9) and that God's goodness and mercy infinitely exceed the worst human sin. That's why I love authors like Dostoyevsky, who stretch us unendurably in both directions: into the Hell within ourselves and into the Heaven within ourselves. I think we are much, much worse and much, much better than we think we are.

That's true at all times. At this particular time and place, I am pessimistic about the culture that used to be called Christendom and is now called Western civilization. It is essentially apostate Christendom. Religion is dying everywhere in this culture — but not anywhere else. Elsewhere in the world, it is defying the predictions of the atheists and growing both in quantity and in quality. So I think if things keep going along the present arcs, we will see a nearly totally materialistic and atheistic culture here and vibrant religious renewals everywhere else, especially in Africa, which is the world's poorest continent and also the world's most religious and the happiest, if you count happiness not by bank accounts but by smiles, which they have the most of, and suicides, which they have the least of. We are the opposite.

Can you say something good about our modern American culture?

Sure. As a philosopher, I see a lot of philosophical wisdom in our culture's popular song titles.

For instance, here is some very practical wisdom from song titles, all in the imperative mood.

- Baby, stop crying
- Cry awhile, cry
- Don't cry
- Keep away from runaround Sue
- Try a little tenderness
- Stand by me
- Help!
- Hark! The herald angels sing
- Don't be cruel
- Let it be
- It ain't no use to sit and wonder why, babe
- Don't worry, be happy
- Mothers, don't let your children grow up to be cowboys
- All of me, why not take all of me?
- Good night, Irene

Ask Peter Kreeft

- God bless America
- Hello, Dolly (how you greet the Dalai Lama)
- Love me or leave me
- Send in the clowns
- Just walk away, Renée
- How you gonna survive unless you get a little crazy?
- Bring it on home to me
- Love me tender
- Love me or leave me
- Take my hand
- I'm a stranger in Paradise

What's the most important thing we can do for our culture? What's the main thing missing?

Those are two different questions. The most important thing we can do for our culture is not to make saving the culture the greatest good, but to know and love and give everything for the real greatest good, ultimate end, and meaning of life. And if you don't know what that is, the first thing for you is to find out.

It's the principle that C. S. Lewis calls the principle of "first and second things." There are many goods, and there is a hierarchy of goods, and if we put second things first and first things second—for instance, if we judge religion by politics instead of politics by religion, or if we see our family as means to ourselves and our happiness rather than seeing ourselves as means to our family—then we will lose both: we will lose not only the first thing that we demoted but also the second thing that we promoted and idolized.

The obvious example of that is addiction. God invented wine to gladden the heart of man, according to the Bible; but when man makes it his end, it saddens rather than gladdens. When we absolutize politics and judge religion by it, we spoil not only religion but also politics. When we see our family as a means to our own happiness, we not only reduce them, but we also reduce ourselves; we lose our happiness, because happiness comes only through unselfishness, never through selfishness.

So with the culture. It's not the first thing. America will not last forever. It is not our eternal home. Washington, D.C., and Harvard and Hollywood will not be in Heaven. You will. Your neighbor will.

What's the main thing missing in our culture? Christ. Our culture is Christophobic. Let Christ come totally into your heart and your life, and He will do the rest. He will seep into your culture through a million pores. There are many good books about some of those pores, and many different opportunities for different people to do different things to help the common good and delay our culture's sickness and death. But the first thing is the real presence of Christ in your soul and in your life, in your thought and in your motives.

Aren't we too fussy about manners?

No. We're not fussy enough.

Manners condition us to morals.

Saying "please" conditions us out of arrogant demands and into humility. Saying "yes, sir" and "yes, ma'am" and "no, sir" and "no, ma'am" conditions us out of egotism and into respect. Saying "thank you" conditions us out of Scroogeyness and into gratitude. Listening politely conditions us not just out of impoliteness and into politeness but also out of selfishness and egotism and into altruism and patience. Keeping our house clean conditions us to keep our lives clean. Keeping our bodies healthy conditions us to keep our souls healthy.

Good manners are like fertilizer. It's not spectacular and exciting, but it's effective — grassroots effective. Start at the bottom, with little things. "The highest does not stand without the lowest."

Plato, in the *Republic*, devised a system of education that was aimed eventually at the Beatific Vision of divine, eternal truth. It began with gymnastic, i.e., exercise, for the body, and music for the most irrational part of the soul, which is also the most powerful part.

Zen Buddhism aims at satori, mystical enlightenment. It begins with posture.

Pets are important for this. Cruelty to animals leads to cruelty to people; *love* of animals conditions us to *love* for people.

Crime rates went significantly down in New York City, especially serious and violent crime rates, when Rudy Giuliani cleaned up the graffiti, garbage, and broken windows on the streets.

It's easier to throw people around if you first throw food around. It's easier to gobble up other people's *lives* if you gobble up your food. It's easier to be sloppy about people if you're sloppy about the silverware.

Yes, the Victorians and the court of King Louis XIV were much too fussy and prissy and picky about manners.

Is that our danger today, or is it the opposite?

Vices always come in opposite pairs.

Why don't people have deep friendships anymore?

I think the biggest reason is that marriage is the greatest friendship, and marriage is in deep trouble.

Marriage counselors often ask couples who are having trouble in their relationships to write down their expectations for each other, thus turning the relationship into a contract. Marriage is not a contract but a covenant; it does not define and limit what each gives to the other. They give themselves whole: soul and body, love and fertility, all their future lives, nothing held back. That's rare today.

Friendship is halfway between a contract and a covenant. It's less than a covenant but more than a contract, unless it's only what Aristotle called a friendship of utility: "Be my friend. I've got a car, and you've got a house; let me sleep in your house, and I'll let you drive my car."

Disappointment always comes from unmet expectations. Don't expect perfection in any human relationship, even marriage, and certainly not in the fake marriage that gives only sex but not life, either in the sense of a lifetime commitment or in the sense of fertility and children and a family. That's a contract.

Prostitution is also a contract. Fake marriage is like free mutual prostitution.

About expectations: the glass of your life is never totally full and never totally empty. Since it's never totally full, your expectations, or at least your hopes, for your spouse or your friend are never totally satisfied. But since it's never totally empty either, there are always things to find and to be grateful for and to praise in your spouse or your friend. If both spouses or friends do this, it's a lot better than a contract. If even one does it thoroughly, even if the other one does it only a little bit, it can change at least one of you (yourself) and change the relationship.

Finite, defined, limited expectations are for contracts, not for real friendships, nonutilitarian friendships. Marriage is the most complete and intimate friendship. If it isn't, it won't work. A marriage that has lost its erotic love but not its friendship can still last and be happy; a marriage that has not lost its eros but has lost its friendship always breaks up miserably.

C. S. Lewis has a very enlightening and controversial chapter on friendship and why it's disappearing in *The Four Loves*. Read it. It's a very wise, practical book. One of his answers to your question of why friendship is rarer today than before is that we're becoming more dependent on the state, and you can't have a friendship with the state. As the state expands, it takes over areas of life that used to be outside its scope, including not only economics and employment but also friendship, marriage, family, and religion.

Don't you think the whole problem is very simple? We're materialists. We identify ourselves with our bodies and we forget our souls.

In one sense, yes. The most practical sentence ever uttered was uttered by the world's greatest economist, the world's greatest expert on profit and loss. The sentence is this: "For what doth it profit a man, if he gain the whole world, and suffer the loss of his own soul?" (Matt. 16:26, Douay-Rheims).

But in another sense, I disagree. The difference between good and evil is not the difference between soul and body, or spirit and matter. All matter is good: God created it. And the evilest thing that exists is a pure spirit, the Devil. Our religion is not "spirituality."

It can't be, because we are not ghosts trapped in machines, spirits trapped in matter, egos trapped in skin bags. We are persons, selves, "I"s that have both bodily and spiritual dimensions, like a book with words and meanings. You can't change the meaning without changing the words, and you can't change the words without changing the meanings.

But Jesus' saying remains true: we can say "I," as animals can't; we can be persons, only because we have spiritual souls, rational souls. We will escape our bodies, for a while, at death, but we can never escape our souls. Your soul can leave its body, but it can't leave itself.

Did you ever think about the fact that you could never escape yourself? It can be a terrifying realization. At every moment, whatever you do and wherever you go, you have to see the whole world from just one narrow perspective: yours. You can't see the world with another person's eyes, or feel the world with his feelings, or think about the world with his thoughts. You are stuck with the company of yourself forever.

It's not just that your ego, self, soul, or mind is trapped in a bag of skin. It's the epidermis of your soul, not of your body, that limits you. Your mind can escape your body, either in mystical experiences, or surfing, or reading an engrossing novel. But your mind can never escape your mind.

And even if it did, it would be *your* mind that escaped your mind. Even if you did escape your prison — whether a prison of stone walls or of your body or of your mind — you cannot escape the escaper. You cannot escape you. X = X.

Something in us rebels against this. That's why there are mystics. That's why our deepest joys are moments when we lose self-consciousness but not life or existence. We want to *be* the others whom we only see.

Perhaps in Heaven we can.

What's your favorite joke?

That's such a profound question that I'm going to make the answer to it the longest answer in the book. Laughter is not only a powerful cause of happiness and an answer to unhappiness; it's also philosophically profound. There is nothing more philosophical than humor. There is nothing more serious than humor. Life is hilariously funny. If you do not understand that, you simply do not understand life. The fact that anything at all exists besides God is very funny. The funniest thing that ever happened was the Incarnation. It was God's greatest joke on the Devil. Chesterton says, at the end of his utterly profound book *Orthodoxy* (which is the most unorthodox book you can imagine), that the thing Jesus hid from his disciples when he abruptly went up a mountain or over the lake — the thing we would understand the least and be the most scandalized about — was probably His laughter.

Tell me your three favorite jokes, and I will know you better than if you tell me your three favorite politicians, foods, drinks, sports, games, singers, scientists, businesses, cities, cars, wild animals, pets, flowers, colors, bands, seasons, or times of day.

So here are my twenty-five favorite jokes. None of them (except one) are original, but jokes are not copyrighted.

Religious jokes

Belfast theology

A man is walking down a dark street in Belfast during the Troubles. Suddenly he finds strong arms surrounding him and a sharp knife at his throat. A nasty voice hisses in his ear: "Tell me quick: Are ye a Protestant, or are ye a Catholic?"

The man thinks: "There's only one way I can get out of here alive." So he answers: "I'm an atheist."

The knife does not move. "A Protestant atheist or a Catholic atheist?"

On the bridge

A Southern Baptist in a Wednesday-night prayer meeting arose and gave this "testimony":

As I was walking to church tonight, I asked God to show me something important I could do for Him. Immediately, I saw ahead of me a man trying to jump off a bridge into the river below. I ran up to him and said, "Don't do it, brother!"

"Why not?" he said.

"Because life is worth living," I said.

"Why?" he asked.

"Because of God," I said. "God is real. And God loves you. You're not an atheist, are you?"

"No," he said.

"Good," I said. "So, what do you believe about God? Are you a Christian, or a Muslim, or a Jew, or what?"

"A Christian," he said.

So I said, "Good! So am I. See? Our God sent me to you, brother. Are you a Protestant Christian or a Catholic Christian?"

"I'm a Protestant," he said.

So I said, "Good! So am I. See? Our God sent me to you, brother. Are you a Baptist or a Methodist or a Presbyterian or a Lutheran, or what?"

"I'm a Baptist," he said.

"So am I!" I said. "See? Our God sent me to you, brother. Are you a Southern Baptist or a Northern Baptist?"

"I'm a Southern Baptist," he said.

"So am I!" I said. "See? Our God sent me to you, brother. Are you a Southern Baptist of the 1898 convention or a Southern Baptist of the 1912 convention?"

"I'm a Southern Baptist of the 1912 convention," he said.

So I said, "Die, heretic!" and I pushed him off the bridge.

The converted bear

A man is out bear hunting when things go seriously wrong. He loses his gun, and a bear spots him and starts to chase him. The bear is very hungry.

The man is a Catholic and believes in miracles, so with the bear about twenty feet behind him, he prays, "Lord, I know You can do miracles. Convert this bear. Turn him into a Catholic."

He turns around to see whether his prayer has been answered. It has. The bear is kneeling and praying. The man smiles, until he hears what the bear is saying:

"Bless us, O Lord, and these Thy gifts which we are about to receive from Thy bounty."

Lawyer jokes

The Devil in Armani

The Devil walks into a lawyer's office wearing an expensive Armani suit.

The lawyer looks up and asks, politely, "What can I do for you, sir?"

The Devil replies, "Oh, no, I'm here because there's something I can do for you. I can make you richer than Bill Gates and more famous than Alan Dershowitz. All you have to do is to sign this little contract, signing over to me your soul and the souls of your wife and your children and your grandchildren for all eternity."

The lawyer narrows his eyes suspiciously, takes the contract, reads it all very carefully, looks up, and says:

"So, what's the catch?"

The barn

A Jew, and Hindu, and a lawyer are out walking together and get lost in the woods. Night comes, and the cold, and they're completely lost and afraid they're going to freeze to death.

Suddenly, they see a light ahead. When they reach it, they find it's the tiny house and barn of a hermit farmer. They knock on the door until they wake him up.

"We're freezing to death; can we sleep in your house tonight?"

"Well, sure. There's a spare room, but it's tiny, and it's got only enough room for two beds in it, so one of you will have to sleep in the barn. But it's nice and warm there too."

"That's OK," says the Jew. "I'll do it. It's my good deed for the day." So the Hindu and the lawyer fall asleep on the beds, and the Jew goes to the barn.

Five minutes later, there's an angry knock at the door. It's the Jew. "There is a pig in that barn. I can't sleep with a pig. That's against my religion. It makes me unclean. Pigs are unclean."

The Hindu says, "Oh, well, I guess it's my karma: I'll sleep in the barn." So, the Jew and the lawyer fall asleep on the beds, and the Hindu goes to the barn.

Five minutes later, there's an angry knock at the door. It's the Hindu. "There is a cow in that barn. I can't sleep with a cow. It's against my religion. Cows are sacred. It makes me unclean."

The lawyer says, "Oh, well, I guess I'll have to sleep in the barn." So the Jew and the Hindu fall asleep on the beds, and the lawyer goes to the barn.

Five minutes later, there are two angry knocks on the door. It's the pig and the cow.

The Pied Piper of San Francisco

A smart New York jeweler is in San Francisco's Chinatown looking for bargains. He sees a tiny, old, musty and dusty basement shop and, on the steps, a tiny, old, musty and dusty Chinese proprietor, who invites the jeweler in. "Come in, come in. Bargains galore here. You want bargain?"

The New Yorker enters and finds the little shop to be crammed full of gold statues: statues of people, of animals, of buildings — everything. And each one has a double price tag.

He picks up a gold statue of a rat, about a foot long. The price tag says: "Rat, $10, story about rat, $10,000." "What does this mean?" he asks.

"It means exactly what it says. You want rat, you pay me ten dollar. You want story about rat, you pay me ten thousand dollar."

"There's a catch, right? I have to buy the story with the rat — is that it?"

"No. You can have rat for ten dollar. But I know you will want to hear story about rat too. Story about rat is worth ten thousand dollar, but rat is only ten dollar."

The New Yorker examines the rat carefully. He thinks: "I know gold when I see it, and this rat is made of solid 14-carat gold. It's not worth ten dollars; it's worth ten thousand dollars.

This guy must have his price tags backward. What an idiot. And what a bargain!" So he plunks down ten dollars, says, "I'm not interested in the story," and walks out with the gold rat under his arm.

Then he hears a sound, the patter of little feet behind him. There is a large rat following him. Then he sees a second rat join the first one, and a third, and a fourth. In a few minutes *every* rat in San Francisco is coming out of the sewers and following him — thousands of rats.

The New Yorker is terrified. He has a phobia about rats; that's why he was drawn to the rat in the shop. He starts to run. The rats also start to run. He runs faster. They also run faster. He is now one block from San Francisco Bay. He has been terrified of rats ever since he was a little kid; that's why his favorite fairy tale was the Pied Piper of Hamelin, in which the Pied Piper has this magic flute and he pipes all the rats of Hamelin into the sea. He is one block from the sea, and his only hope is that there is some truth in that fairy tale. So, he runs to the edge of the water, the rats only a few feet behind him, and he throws the gold rat into the sea. And all the rats follow the gold rat and drown themselves in the sea. He is now the Pied Piper of San Francisco, who has saved the whole city from its rats.

He sits on the dock thinking about this, as the bodies of dead rats drift past him one by one. He struggles with himself and finally gives up. He goes back to the Chinese shop. There's the proprietor sitting on the steps as before. "Aha. You are back. I knew you will come back. You want story about rat now, no?"

"No," says the New Yorker. And he starts looking over the thousands of statues.

"Oh? Why you come back then? What you looking for?"

"I was hoping you might have a gold lawyer."

Jokes about men and women

The real story of Adam and Eve

God created Eve first and said to her, "Are you lonely?"

"Yes," she said.

"Well, I've got a terrific solution to that. I'm going to create a man for you."

"What's a man?"

"Oh, he's a knight in shining armor, and he'll slay dragons for you. He's tall, dark, and handsome, and he'll open stuck jar lids for you."

"That sounds too good to be true," said Eve. "Is there a catch?"

"Of course," said God. "There's always a catch."

"So what's the catch?"

"He's going to have a big, big ego. So we're all going to have to play this little game and pretend that I created him *first*."

The alternative version of the Adam and Eve story

God created Adam first, and said, "Are you lonely?"

Adam said, "Yes."

"Well, I've got a terrific solution to that. I'm going to create a woman for you."

"What's a woman?"

"She's my masterpiece. She's the most beautiful thing in the universe. She'll be great in bed. She'll cook for you and clean for you and take care of your babies, and she'll be madly in love with you and adore you and obey you and never even complain at you."

"Wow," said Adam. "That sounds too good to be true. Is there a catch?"

"Of course," said God. "There's always a catch."

"It's gonna cost me something, right?"

"Right."

"How much is it gonna cost me?"

"Oh, it's gonna cost you an arm and a leg."

"What can I get for a rib?"

The talking frog

An old man walking past a pond hears a frog talking to him. "Pick me up, please!"

The man picks him up, and the frog says, "I am a beautiful princess who has been turned into a frog. If you kiss me, you will break the spell, and I will use my charms of body and soul to fulfill your every wish."

The man says nothing and puts the frog in his coat pocket. "Didn't you hear what I said?" says the frog.

"Yes, I heard you. But at my age, a talking frog is more exciting than a beautiful woman."

Man's best friend

Why do they call a dog a man's best friend? Shouldn't his wife be his best friend?

Well, let's see. Let's do a scientific experiment to find out who is man's best friend.

Lock your dog and your wife in the trunk of your car for an hour and then let them out, and you'll see which one is your best friend.

Mrs. Moses

Why were the Children of Israel wandering in the wilderness for forty years?

Because Moses wouldn't stop and ask for directions.

He also wouldn't let Mrs. Moses drive.

What's your favorite joke?

The death sentence

Abe is getting old and hasn't had a general exam in years because he's afraid of doctors.

Mabel, his wife, persuades him to go.

She privately tells the doctor: "If there's anything wrong with him, please tell me first and let me tell him. He's scared of doctors."

The doctor agrees, examines Abe, and meets privately with Mabel.

"Your husband has a weak heart. He can't take frustration. The only way to keep him alive is never to cross him or argue with him or complain at him. And give him whatever pleasures he wants."

On the way home, Abe asks Mabel what the doctor said.

Mabel replies, "You're gonna die."

Philosophy jokes

The most-asked question for a philosopher

What question will a philosophy major ask most often for the rest of his life?

"You want fries with that?"

The mixed marriage

What happens when a godfather marries a deconstructionist?

Their kids learn to make them an offer they can't understand.

Philosopher versus pizza

What's the difference between a philosopher and a large pizza?

A large pizza can feed a family of four.

265

The philosopher in the zoo

A philosopher can find no work, so he goes to the zoo and asks if they have any jobs there.

The zookeeper says, "The only thing I have is a temporary job. Our gorilla just died, and the replacement won't arrive for three months, so if you get a gorilla suit and go in the cage and act like a real gorilla, and if you convince the public that you're the real thing, I'll pay you for three months."

The philosopher has no other prospects, so he does it.

The first day is a total failure. Everybody laughs at him. At the end of the day, the zookeeper is ready to fire him, but the philosopher pleads for one more chance, and he gets it.

The second day, he really goes ape, and everybody believes he's real. He climbs the tree in his cage, but the branch breaks, and he falls into the adjoining cage, where there is a lion.

The lion looks skinny and hungry (the recession has been bad for everybody) and starts to stalk him.

The philosopher tries to think logically: "If I call out for help, I'll probably be saved, but I'll certainly lose my job. If I don't call out for help, I'll probably be eaten, but I'll die because I was a success in imitating a gorilla, not a failure."

By this time, the lion is almost touching him. He decides to call for help and opens his mouth.

Too late!

The lion lifts a paw and puts it over his mouth; then he puts his mouth to the philosopher's ear and says, "Shut up, you fool, you're not the only philosopher out of work."

The politically incorrect operation

To reconcile conservative and liberal philosophers, an experimental operation was tried: a mutual heart and brain transplant.

But it didn't work because they couldn't find any conservative who would give his heart to a liberal, and they couldn't find a liberal who had any brains to give to a conservative, since they were all so open-minded that their brains fell out.

Sherlock Holmes's lesson in deduction

Holmes and Watson are out camping overnight.

At three in the morning, Holmes wakes Watson and says: "Tell me what you see."

"I see the stars."

"Yes," says Holmes. "So tell me what you deduce from what you see."

"I deduce that the universe is full of great beauty, and that there is a cosmic intelligence pervading all things, and that—"

"No, no, you idiot."

"What else?"

"Somebody has stolen our tent!"

The worst pun in the world

The real story of the execution of John the Baptist

You know the Bible story of the beheading of John the Baptist by King Herod at the request of Salome the dancing girl, who so pleased the king that he promised to give her anything she wanted. She asked her mother what to ask for, and her mother said, "The head of John the Baptist." Well, this is the rest of the story.

Salome and her mother were from Genoa, Italy, where they had owned an Italian deli. When Salome asked for the head of John the Baptist, the ax man was sick, so Herod looked around for a substitute, and the only man in his court who could chop off a head was his provost, who used to be an ax man before he became the provost.

But he agreed to do it because he was a good friend of Herod. In fact, Herod called him by his nickname, "Prov."

But the provost protested to Herod, "I know this guy John. He's tough. He has a thick neck."

Herod replied, "Heads will roll: either his if you do it, or yours if you don't."

"It will be his head that rolls," said the provost, "but he is tough. It will be a hard job."

When Salome heard this conversation, she wanted to go with the provost to the execution.

Her mother insisted on coming with her, but Salome said to her, "No, Mother. Remember what you taught me back at our deli: 'Genoa Salome goes with prov alone on a hard roll.'"

Surfing

Do you still surf?

Does the pope still pray?

Do fish still swim?

There's no such thing as an ex-surfer.

I don't surf much because I live near Lake Atlantic. That means I learn patience, one of life's most precious and difficult arts. The expression "Surf's up" is supposed to be typically Californian, but it isn't, because that's not news; the surf is *usually* up in the Pacific. "Surf's up" in California is like "Sun's out" in Hawaii. But it's news on the East Coast.

I've been asked whether there are any waves in Massachusetts. I assure you, there are. I actually saw one; I think it was in 1978.

What's the big deal about surfing?

Stoke.

The big deal is stoke.

Many things give you a "high," but the high that comes from surfing has its own name, "stoke." It's the unique joy you get when you've caught a good wave, and the joy that comes from everything that surrounds it, especially the sea itself.

There are many other joys in life, and each one has a different quality. But stoke is the paradox of total freedom through conforming to the wave, becoming yourself by losing yourself in the wave. It's paradoxical in many ways: not only is it freedom through conformity, but it's also excitement and at the same time peace.

It's a foretaste of Heaven, where we will surf on God. And it's an icon of the ultimate purpose and meaning of life on earth, which is being a saint, the essence of which is unselfish, self-forgetful love of God and neighbor. A wave is a kind of holy picture, an icon, of the will of God.

Is that enough?

You're a fake. You're not a surfer; you use a boogie board, a sponge. You're a sponger.

Am I a fake reader because I read printed books instead of hand-written books, because I take advantage of Gutenberg's great invention of the printing press?

Well, George Morey, the inventor of the boogie board, or bodyboard, was one of the great inventors of all time. Like Gutenberg, he took one of life's greatest joys, which used to be available only to a small, select few, the young and athletic, and made it available to everybody.

To be a stand-up surfer, especially on a shortboard (a longboard is easier), you have to be fairly athletic, and have a decent sense of balance. And it takes quite a lot of practice, a lot of time and effort, to do it well.

But anybody can learn to use a bodyboard, even old fogies with a balance problem, like me. And you can do pretty much everything with a bodyboard that you can do with a stand-up surfboard.

It takes a while to learn just how to judge the wave: whether it's the right size to catch—it can be too little or too big (but even too-big ones can be caught not as they break but after they break, when the white foam rolls in).

The best breaks for beginners are ones where the drop-off is gradual, so you can go out fairly far without your feet leaving the ground, so you can jump onto the wave just as it breaks on you, in what's called the impact zone — like catching a moving train or jumping on a horse on a moving merry-go-round. You can also use swim fins and swim into the wave as it breaks in deeper water, but that takes a little more practice and athletic effort, and, of course, stronger swimming ability if you're going out into water that's over your head.

The canard about spongers comes from the fact that the bodyboards they give to little kids usually have a spongy, soft bottom, and they don't give you a good ride. The best bodyboards are the ones with smooth, rigid bottoms, especially the ones that are a little longer than the average bodyboard. If you pay under a hundred dollars for a bodyboard, you're either compromising on quality or getting a bargain.

Bodyboards are for almost everybody. If everybody was bodyboarding, nobody would be murdering or terrorizing or plotting revolutions. The bodyboard is the answer to how to get world peace. If Hitler had been a bodyboarder, he wouldn't have had to invent the war to find his stoke.

Miscellany

What is the secret of your success as a writer?

What secret? What success? It's a bad question.

If there is any success and any secret, it is at least to a great extent in my handicap, which is my ADD. It makes me bored very quickly and too lazy to persist at long, difficult intellectual tasks that are boring, such as detailed scholarship. I don't have my nose in a book, my body in a library, or my eyes on a computer screen for hours at a time. That means I will never write a great work of philosophical or theological scholarship. But I will write simple, short books that don't bore readers because they don't bore me.

Most philosophers are more intelligent than I am. They often make poor teachers because very few students can understand them. I thank God I'm only a little more intelligent than most of my students and most of my readers. If you think *I'm* too abstract and head-in-the-clouds, you haven't met many other philosophers.

I'm serious about this handicap business. I never met anyone who didn't have some kind of handicap, some kind of minus, some lack of a talent or power or virtue (such as patience) that most people have. I think we can learn that important truth best from people who are more obviously handicapped: we can learn from them who we are. We are all the handicapped.

We are also the talented. I never met anyone who did not have some talent that I do not have.

God made everybody different, so that every one of us can do two things: we can look up in admiration to somebody who's better than we are at something, and we can look down in love and compassion to somebody who's worse, and we can teach him and help him. Those are two of life's greatest joys: being a student and being a teacher, being an apprentice and being a master, being helped and being a helper, being a receiver and being a giver. Surely these two great gifts will continue in Heaven. We will not be equal in Heaven, because if we were, we would lose those two great opportunities: admiration and active compassion. Hurrah for hierarchy!

Of course, this fact of hierarchy and inequality also makes possible great sins and great perversions, throughout history, and we all know what they are. But great perversions and great versions always go together. It's the lilies that fester that smell far worse than weeds. Free will and intelligence are gifts that make us closer to God than the animals, but they also make sin and even Hell possible. When you see a great perversion, like a Hitler, look for some version, some power, some talent, that could have been used for great good. Imagine Hitler straightened out into a saint!

So, we all have two secrets: our special ability and our special disability. Our parents and teachers are always telling us about the first secret, especially if we are young and unsure of ourselves. Our spouses and our children and our siblings are always telling us about the second secret, our disability, especially when we goof or act up. They are both right.

I guess I am a successful writer because I am good at words, at reading them and remembering them and inventing them, and above all loving them. But I am very bad about numbers, especially about anything digital. I cannot wrap my mind around the meaning of computer language, though I've tried for decades. I'm also forgetful, absentminded, and clumsy about anything mechanical, and I can't do two things at once, such as picking out one voice in a crowded restaurant.

My daughter is the opposite. She has to ask me how to write a letter, but she's a whiz at anything digital, and she understands intuitively how things work and how to fix them.

I have to ask her to turn on the TV for me when it refuses to obey me. Digital things always obey her, like tamed and trained circus animals, or like the Sea of Galilee when Christ stilled the storm by saying to it: "Peace! Be still!" (I translate that as "Down, Fido!")

It's very good that we all have handicaps. God dearly loves every one of His brain-damaged children, as He watches us hold each other up like drunks who would otherwise collapse. A world of identical geniuses would be unendurable. As a philosophy professor who loves Plato, I sometimes fantasize about a world of seven billion Platos. And then my fantasy turns to a shudder.

And here is a corollary of the fact that we are all failures at something.

We are all failures at different things, which makes both admiration and compassionate help possible, as I said; but we are also all failures at the same thing, which is the most important thing of all, the point and purpose and meaning and end and design of our lives—namely, being saints, being loving and wise and unselfish and full of joy. (And the saints are the most adamantly clear and insistent about that. As Pascal says, there are only two kinds of people: saints, who say they are sinners, and sinners, who say they are saints.)

So we are all failures. But we can be happy and hopeful failures instead of either satisfied failures or miserable failures.

There are only four possibilities:

1. I'm not a failure at all. I'm perfect. I'm a god.
2. I'm a satisfied failure. I'm perfect in my imperfection. I have no aspirations.
3. I'm a miserable failure because I'm hopeless. I stink. I hate myself.
4. I'm a hopeful, humble, happy failure because God loves me anyway and promises to fix me and happify me. He's crazy. Life is crazy, funny, weird, and wonderful.

Only that fourth philosophy explains humor. It's not "comic relief" from life, an escape from life, an oasis in the desert of life. It's a philosophy of life. It's the only true philosophy of life.

Who laughs the most?

Babies. Watch them.

What do they laugh at?

Everything!

When we were as wise as that, we understood, intuitively, that life is a crazy, wonderful mystery. That's why we were instinctively religious; in fact, we were mystical. No one is born an atheist; we become atheists when we become cynical, and we become cynical when we start to see life as a series of bothersome, troublesome problems, and we stop laughing.

We are all babies to God. He holds us in His arms and laughs back at us as we look up at His face and laugh. Look at that look on the face of a baby who's looking up at the face of his mother or father.

What do you see in that look?

What is the secret of your success as a writer?

You see four things: faith, hope, love, and the fact that those three are really one thing. You see that more clearly in babies' smiles than anywhere else.

Who smiles the most?

Those who have Down syndrome.

They may have less problem-solving intelligence, but they have more wisdom and more happiness.

What continent smiles the most?

Africa, the poorest continent in the world. Whenever you see Africans, they're smiling.

Who smiles the least?

Scandinavians.

Now, there are three things Scandinavians rate the highest in and Africans rate the lowest in: incomes; clean, orderly, disease-free physical environments with plenty of good medical care; and rational, reliable, stable, orderly political structures that give every citizen security in a welfare state.

That's why the Global Happiness Project picked the five Scandinavian countries as the happiest counties in the world and five sub-Saharan African countries as the unhappiest.

But they forgot two other things, things any idiot knows are surer indications of happiness and unhappiness than anything else: smiles and suicides.

Even babies, who don't know a single word, recognize happiness when they see it in a smile. They smile back and laugh. Only an expert could possibly ignore that.

And here's a second indication that's so obvious that only an expert could ignore it: suicide. Smiles prove happiness; suicide proves unhappiness.

Now, who smiles more, those dour Africans or those sunny, smiling Scandinavians? And where is the suicide rate the highest, in Africa or in Scandinavia?

Some things are so obvious that only an expert could miss them.

In light of your last answer, don't you believe in autonomy?

No.

Why not?

Because it's not true. (That's the only honest reason for not believing in anything, by the way. And the reason is more important than the conclusion. I think an honest atheist has a better chance at Heaven than a dishonest theist, because God is Truth, and if you don't love Truth, you don't love God, and you wouldn't enjoy God in Heaven.)

Why isn't autonomy true?

Because God is Truth but God is not autonomy. God is Trinity. So God is not an American.

Indeed not.

Americans used to believe in truth. Now they believe in autonomy.

What do you mean by that?

I mean that according to the most popular religion in America, pop psychology, there are currently 350 million autonomous godlike beings who invent their own truth, who equate truth with what's "true for me."

Where did that idea come from? Why is it so typically American?

I don't know. I suspect it had something to do with our founding. We fought a war against being England's nonautonomous colony. "Live free or die" is still the motto of one of our original states (New Hampshire). That's fine in politics, especially when you are the rebels against the king, but it's fatally easy for us to feel the same way about King God as we did about King George.

The atheist poet wrote: "I am the master of my fate; I am the captain of my soul." Most Americans *don't* call themselves atheists, but they believe that line, and that's practical atheism. And that's popular. Why else would everyone love Frank Sinatra's song "I Did It My Way"? He even imagines singing that when he dies. And people find that moving. It moves you, all right: it moves you right to Hell. That's the song they all sing as they enter Hell. That was the Devil's philosophy: "Better to reign in Hell than to serve in Heaven." It moves me, all right: it gives me a bowel movement.

Someone who believes that song has forgotten the two most important words they learned when they were two years old: "please" and "thank you."

You said we are not autonomous. Does that mean we are dependent?

Yes. This is not a theory; it is a fact. Whenever you ride in a car or use a computer, remember that it is not you. It is not part of your identity. The computer is not an extension of your brain, and the car is not an extension of your legs. It's a machine. It's a slave that's not made of flesh and blood. If it's stolen, you are not diminished; you are still whole.

When you breathe, or eat, or drink, or exercise, remember that it is your body; i.e., it is you using your body to do all these things. Your body is not doing it without your soul, either consciously or unconsciously. Corpses do nothing.

You own not only your machines and your body's fuel (food and drink) and even your body itself in a sense (a strange sense: your body is you, so it is both owner and owned; you own yourself), but you also "own" your mind. It's "your" mind, after all. You are more than all these things put together.

If you can "lose your mind," you must be more than your mind, just as if you can lose your body (at death), you must be more than your body.

Therefore, you are independent of all these things. Recognize your independence.

But also recognize your dependence — on your Creator for your very existence, not just in the moment when you came into existence but at every moment, including the present moment. If God stopped willing your existence, you would disappear. The only possible ultimate source of your being is Being Itself. You are to Him what Hamlet is to Shakespeare.

The two great commandments are really one. Obedience to either one involves obedience to the other. So, there are only two kinds of people: people who believe there are only two kinds of people and people who don't. No, that's just a joke. But there really are only two kinds of people. C. S. Lewis said it perfectly: "There are only two kinds of people, in the end: those who say to God, 'Thy will be done' and those to whom God says, in the end, 'Thy will be done.'" Rotate the picture ninety degrees, from vertical to horizontal, and you can see the difference: There are givers, and there are getters.

That's why parenting is the best moral training in the world. Parents are naturally givers, and kids are naturally getters.

Some adults remain kids all their lives.

We live in a youth culture that tells you to expect fun and freedom into your twenties and thirties. Old age, middle age, and parenting are seen as a bummer and a boredom and a prison. In other words, our culture makes us spoiled brats. When you're young, people tolerate your being a brat, i.e., being a getter instead of a giver, i.e., living for your own pleasure, i.e., being selfish, as long as you're *politely* selfish. You're not expected to be *good*, just *nice*.

You teach at Boston College.
Is BC still Catholic?

Yes. As the students say, "BC" stands for "Barely Catholic."

Seriously, I love BC. I've been there for over fifty years. It's a great combination for me: it's Catholic enough to feel like home, and it's pagan enough to be mission territory.

Would you recommend that I send my kid to BC?

Yes, if your kid is a strong Catholic. And if you have the money.

Franciscan University of Steubenville and Ave Maria University and Belmont Abbey and the University of Dallas and Christendom College and, above all, Thomas Aquinas College are all both cheaper and more orthodox, but BC has many things they don't have, as a big city has many things that a good, comfortable small town doesn't have.

It all depends on the individual. A smart, mature, non-naive, thoughtful Catholic student can get an excellent education at BC, both academically and religiously, if he knows which teachers and courses to take and which friends to make and which student organizations to join. But if his faith is weak and wobbly when he enters, it will very probably disappear entirely by the time he graduates. As with all the Jesuit colleges I know, BC's bottom line, the end product, is double: BC makes a few very good Catholics out of non-Catholics, and it also makes a lot of non-Catholics out of weak Catholics. It makes some strong Catholics out of weak Catholics, but it also makes some weak Catholics out of strong Catholics.

No non-Catholic university does the positive half of that, and it's worth spending the outrageous tuition money for your kids' minds and souls, which are priceless.

BC is also a happy place. Nearly everybody here is happy with it, and that's something that cannot be said of most universities. No infighting, no nastiness, no intrigues, no "us versus them" mentality. It's big but it's like a big family. Quite apart from their sometimes-questionable theological orthodoxy, the Jesuits are very good at caring for people, for individuals.

So, is BC Catholic, or is it Jesuit?

Where do you live?

New York.

So let me ask you: Are you an American, or are you a New Yorker?

I can interpret that in two ways. Are you saying that New York is part of America, so the Jesuits are part of the Catholic Church? Or are you saying that New Yorkers aren't really Americans and Jesuits aren't really Catholics?

You could interpret that either way.

What way do you interpret it?

Well, let's do a little logic. If New York is part of America, all New Yorkers are Americans, but not all Americans are New Yorkers. So, if Jesuits are a part of the Catholic Church, all Jesuits are Catholics.

But some New Yorkers are not good Americans.

Right. And some Jesuits are good Catholics, and some are bad Catholics, but all are Catholics.

Ask Peter Kreeft

Seriously, what's with the Jesuits, anyway?

Seriously, the same thing that's wrong with you and me. We're sinners—and often stupid, shallow, even stinky sinners. Welcome to the world east of Eden.

You're avoiding the question. Why are Jesuit colleges full of heretics? Heretics seem to be drawn to their theology departments as Irishmen are drawn to bars or academics to bookstores.

Jesuits are very smart and well trained. I admire them. Some of the people I admire the most in the world are Jesuits. Many of the best theologians I know are Jesuits, such as John Courtney Murray and John Hardon and Norris Clarke, under whom I studied philosophy at Fordham: an absolutely stellar philosopher and, I think, a real saint. On the other hand, many of our heretics are Jesuits.

Oops, sorry, that word can't be used any more; it's "hate speech." (I mean the word "heretics," not the word "Jesuits.") We now call them "dissenters." We also call the Ten Commandments "values" and sins "lifestyle choices." Not sure what the politically correct substitute for Hell is. Probably "compulsory PC sensitivity training."

Fulton Sheen advised parents to send their kids to Catholic colleges if they were in the market for the most likely path to *losing* their faith. Only half as many graduating seniors identify as Catholics as do entering freshmen, so you see what he meant in terms of the product of most so-called Catholic higher education. As the most practical man who ever lived one said, "By their fruits you shall know them" (Matt. 7:16, Douay-Rheims). What applies to Catholic colleges in general applies to Jesuit colleges particularly.

But not all of us are heretics. Some of us are still politically incorrect. And there are a lot of us left at BC, especially in the Philosophy Department, which I very highly recommend.

I guess the reason there are both so many very good Jesuits and so many very bad Jesuits is the same reason there are so many New Yorkers: there are just so many. There are many wonderful things in New York and also so many awful things in New York, because it's so big.

I love the heart of Jesuit spirituality: finding God everywhere, finding the sacred in the secular.

That's our task, our "great commission." On the other hand, that's dangerous because the secular can easily swallow up the sacred. When you send saints into whorehouses, two things will probably happen: some of the saints will convert the whores, and some of them will be converted by the whores. (I don't mean literal whorehouses but bastions of secular, anti-Christian thought and culture. Two of the biggest whorehouses in America are Hollywood and Harvard.)

What is the best college for philosophy?

Good question. I will not give a safe, polite answer, or nuance it or shuffle around it or hem and haw. It's Thomas Aquinas College in Santa Paula, California. Every person I ever met who graduated from there has impressed me as being truly educated. But that's all they do: they make you thoughtful, wise, fair, and reasonable, and they educate you both academically and religiously. They don't train you for specializations. They don't make you narrow; they make you broad.

All the little start-up Catholic Great Books colleges are good that way: Wyoming Catholic College, and Catholic College of the South and Thomas More College and John Paul the Great College. And some big ones are great: Franciscan University of Steubenville and Ave Maria University and Christendom College, and a few others too, such as the University of Dallas and Belmont Abbey. Some Protestant colleges are Catholic friendly, such as Baylor and the King's College in New York City, where I teach part-time.

Notre Dame is like BC. You can get a good Catholic education there if you really want to, and you can also get lost there in political correctness. But neither BC nor Notre Dame are half as bad as Georgetown. Go there only if you want to get prestige, prosperity, power, and pragmatism.

Ask Peter Kreeft

It's increasingly hard to find good programs in the humanities, especially outside of Catholic colleges. I read a study a few years ago that said that 99.4 percent of the research-and-development budget of all the universities in America is now devoted to science and technology (the STEM courses) and only 0.6 percent for all the humanities and the arts. Nobody nowadays wants to pay big tuition money for wisdom, only for something that will make more money. We're more in love with making cash than making kids. We want our money to get pregnant, but not our women. We treat money like sex, and we treat sex like money because we use sex to sell things in sexy advertising. In other words, we are upside down. One of the things good philosophy has to do is to turn us right side up. That's why I love G.K. Chesterton: he's a master at that.

How can we appreciate everything's preciousness?

Get cancer.

When the doctor tells you your days are numbered, you begin to see every blade of grass as beautiful.

Doctor God has already pronounced that diagnosis, but we don't take Him seriously. We forget that He is not so much a preacher as a scientist. We don't "number our days, and so get wisdom" (Ps. 90:12, Douay-Rheims).

People usually become quite wise and profound on their deathbeds. We are on our deathbeds as soon as we are born. We give birth crouching over a grave.

That's one way: look at the future. Nothing will be here forever. Another way is to look at the past: once upon a time, nothing that we see here now was there at all. Everything is an achievement, a conquest of nothingness, an event, a thing that did not have to be and therefore that once was not. It's a gift. Thank God for it, for everything, even hemorrhoids. Corpses don't have them.

How important are pets?

More important than we think. For many of us, they are the best early-childhood training in life's most important lessons, love and responsibility. They're easy to love, and we need the easy lessons first.

Obviously, sanctity doesn't come easy. It's many steps up the ladder from loving a dog. But God stoops to conquer. He's not proud. He shows us His back before He shows us His face. He's also a punster. "Dog" is "God" backward. In a sense, so is everything else.

What's the hardest question
you were ever asked?

I taught Dostoyevsky's *The Brothers Karamazov* in a Philosophy in Literature class. It's the greatest novel ever written, and certainly the most Christian and the most profound. It takes the reader and shakes him up by showing him both the Heaven and the Hell in his own soul. It's full of darkness and sin and evil and depravity and hate and despair and insanity, but it's even more full of brilliant light and passionate love and saintly goodness, especially God's mercy.

A girl in the front row who never asked a question throughout the course came up to me after the course was over and said, "Do you believe all this stuff? I mean all the stuff Dostoyevsky believes?"

"Yes, I do."

"About the love of God, I mean. About how crazy much God loves us stupid sinners?"

"Absolutely."

"Why?"

"Why do I believe it? Because ..."

"No, I'm not asking for arguments. I mean why does God do it? Why does God love us so much?"

I was stumped and stunned by the question. So, I did what clever cowards do: I avoided the question. "I dunno. Ask me next year. Maybe I'll know then."

It was a stupid answer, but she took is so seriously that one year later, she showed up in the same classroom after the final exam, where I was teaching the same course again.

"Do you remember me?"

"Yes, I do. You asked me that great question about *The Brothers K.* after the last class. And I told you to come back in a year, and here you are. You're still asking that question, I see. Wonderful! I am impressed."

"So, do you have an answer?"

"No, I don't think anybody will ever have that answer in this world. That's one of the reasons we've got to get to Heaven."

She smiled. "OK," she said.

About the Author

Peter Kreeft, Ph.D., is a professor of philosophy at Boston College and also at the King's College in New York City. He is a regular contributor to several Christian publications, is in wide demand as a speaker at conferences, and is the author of more than seventy-five books. Dr. Kreeft is a convert to the Catholic Church from Reformed Protestantism. He earned an A.B. degree from Calvin College, an M.A. and Ph.D. from Fordham University, followed by postdoctoral work at Yale University. He has received several honors for achievements in the field of philosophy, including the Woodrow Wilson Award, Yale-Sterling Fellowship, Newman Alumni Scholarship, Danforth Asian Religions Fellowship, and a Wethersfield–Homeland Foundation Fellowship.

Sophia Institute

Sophia Institute is a nonprofit institution that seeks to nurture the spiritual, moral, and cultural life of souls and to spread the Gospel of Christ in conformity with the authentic teachings of the Roman Catholic Church.

Sophia Institute Press fulfills this mission by offering translations, reprints, and new publications that afford readers a rich source of the enduring wisdom of mankind.

Sophia Institute also operates the popular online resource CatholicExchange.com. *Catholic Exchange* provides world news from a Catholic perspective as well as daily devotionals and articles that will help readers to grow in holiness and live a life consistent with the teachings of the Church.

In 2013, Sophia Institute launched Sophia Institute for Teachers to renew and rebuild Catholic culture through service to Catholic education. With the goal of nurturing the spiritual, moral, and cultural life of souls, and an abiding respect for the role and work of teachers, we strive to provide materials and programs that are at once enlightening to the mind and ennobling to the heart; faithful and complete, as well as useful and practical.

Sophia Institute gratefully recognizes the Solidarity Association for preserving and encouraging the growth of our apostolate over the course of many years. Without their generous and timely support, this book would not be in your hands.

www.SophiaInstitute.com
www.CatholicExchange.com
www.SophiaInstituteforTeachers.org

Sophia Institute Press® is a registered trademark of Sophia Institute.
Sophia Institute is a tax-exempt institution as defined by the
Internal Revenue Code, Section 501(c)(3). Tax ID 22-2548708.